GOLDEN GOA

CANADIAN CATALOGUING IN PUBLICATION DATA

Buday, Grant, 1956–
Golden Goa

ISBN 1-55022-412-3

1. Buday, Grant, 1956– — Journeys — India. 2. Camöens, Luis de, 1524?–1580 —
Journeys — India. 3. Goa (India : State) — Description and travel.
4. Portuguese — India — Goa (State). 5. India — Description and travel. I. Title.

DS498.B82 2000   915.4'799   C00-930441-X

A misFit book edited by Michael Holmes
Cover and text design by Tania Craan
Author photo by Eden Evans
Cover photo by Photonica
Layout by Mary Bowness
Printed by Marc Veilleux

Distributed in Canada by General Distribution Services,
325 Humber Blvd., Toronto, Ontario M9W 7C3

Published by ECW PRESS
2120 Queen Street East, Suite 200,
Toronto, Ontario, M4E 1E2
www.ecw.ca/press

The publication of *Golden Goa* has been generously
supported by The Canada Council, the Ontario Arts Council,
and the Government of Canada through the Book Publishing
Industry Development Program. Canadä

GOLDEN GOA

Grant Buday

MISFIT

ECW PRESS

To Eden

Now, after travelling some eight thousand miles around the country, I know approximately as little as I did on my first arrival. However, I've seen a lot of people and places, and at least I have a somewhat more detailed and precise idea of my ignorance than I did in the beginning.

Paul Bowles

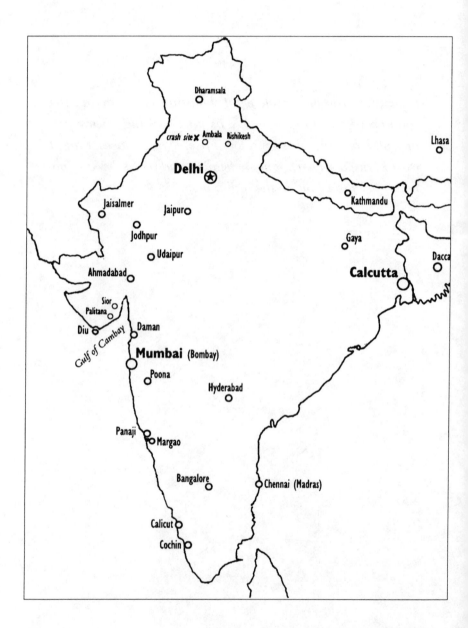

Dharamsala

crash site ✕ Ambala Rishikesh

Lhasa

Delhi ✪

Jaisalmer   Jaipur

Kathmandu

Jodhpur   Gaya

Udaipur

Dacca

Ahmadabad   **Calcutta**

Sior
Palitana

Diu   Daman

Gulf of Cambay

Mumbai (Bombay)

Poona

Hyderabad

Panaji
Margao

Bangalore   Chennai (Madras)

Calicut

Cochin

INTRODUCTION

It took me five trips to India to gather the material for *Golden Goa*. At first I didn't even know I was writing a book. I was just travelling. I wandered the streets, sat in bad hotel rooms, and thought how much better it'd be somewhere else. When in India I thought I should be in Mexico; in Mexico I thought I should be in Europe; in Europe I thought I should be back in India. In Lisbon, in 1981, I made the connection between Portugal and India. I was in the Alfama, Lisbon's Old Quarter, which overlooks the comparatively sleepy harbour. The first Europeans to establish a colony in India set sail from that harbour. And while colonial conquest is not admirable, the seamanship was. I once sailed from Fiji to New Zealand, and I turned out to be a pretty useless sailor. Maybe that's why the sixteenth-century Portuguese impressed me. They'd made it all the way around Africa and across to India in ships as short as a city bus. My interest in India renewed. I returned there in the fall of 1983, but instead of visiting Goa I got into a train crash in which sixteen people died. After that I didn't travel for seven years, not because I was traumatized, but because I was twenty-seven and had to "get serious."

Then one night, alone in my room that overlooked an alley, I was studying the atlas. It was 1990, I was bored with being serious, and desperate to escape the rut of depression caused by my recent divorce. Seeking escape via my 1963 *Reader's Digest* atlas, I found the island of Diu. Diu was as tiny as its name, a dot off the southern tip of Gujarat. It had also been a

Portuguese colony. Until 1961, the Portuguese still controlled three territories in India: Goa, Daman, and Diu. Everyone knew of Goa's beaches and hippies, but what of Daman, and what of Diu? I looked in guidebooks and found little. I dug into histories and found less. That was frustrating but also exciting. Diu in particular interested me. It was an obscure island in an even more obscure location. Diu felt like a discovery. My boredom vanished because I now had a direction.

Inspired, I read everything I could about Portuguese India. I learned of Luis de Camoens (Cam-oosh), author of *The Lusiads*, the Portuguese national epic. Camoens spent eleven years in India in the 1500s. He was a poet, courtier, soldier, and sailor known for his moodiness, the latter quality something I identified with. Heartbroken over an unattainable woman, he got exiled to India for his part in a sword fight. His life took root in my imagination. That's when my travels in India became research.

I returned to India in 1990 and went to Diu, Daman, and Goa. Luis de Camoens was never far from my mind. In 1992, I returned again, then once more in 1998, each time thinking of Camoens, each time getting answers to the questions that were raised on the previous visit. The answers always surprised me. Every Catholic Goan I met, for example, missed the Portuguese. As one fellow put it, "With the Portuguese we meant something. With India we're nothing." I often wondered what a man like Camoens, for whom life in India was a miserable state of limbo, would think of that.

Those five visits to India spanned twenty years, from 1978 to 1998. The country changed. Bombay became Mumbai;

Madras became Chennai. The crowding worsened, the air turned grey with pollution, and television, another form of pollution, was suddenly everywhere. Once, in a four-dollar room in Simla, I turned on the TV, and there was Phil Donahue discussing masturbation. Now what would Camoens think of that?

ONE

The animals felt it first. The skittishness of the cats and the sows alerted the sailors who checked the horizon. Before the black clouds even appeared, they knew a storm was coming. The wind increased. Darkness hit, and the gale threw the Sao Bento *onto her side. The year was 1553. They were off the Cape of Storms, recently renamed the Cape of Good Hope, and among the hundreds hunkering beneath the oak deck was Luis de Camoens, twenty-nine years old, newly released from prison, and on his way to exile in India for stabbing one Gonçalo Borges. The exile was supposed to last three years, but Camoens would not return to Portugal for seventeen.*

Camoens had been a rising star in Lisbon, a poet and playwright who'd been welcomed by the royal family. Then everything fell apart. He lost an eye in the army, and then he lost the love of his life, Catherine de Ataide.

Catherine's father forbade her to marry the penniless Camoens, and so, drunk and miserable one night, the distraught lover stabbed Gonçalo Borges, who was getting the better of two of Camoens's friends in a sword fight. The red-bearded Camoens was always lean, but he would get even leaner after eight months in the notorious Tronco prison, where prisoners were kept chained to tree stumps. Camoens was released on condition of doing military service in India. How ironic that his epic poem, The Lusiads, *which glorifies Portuguese history and exploration, would be written in exile far from the very country he celebrated.*

Luis de Camoens

DELHI 1989

Like all the *naos*, or "great ships," that sailed from Portugal, the one carrying Camoens would have been infested with rats. Nearly 450 years later, I felt a peculiar kinship with Camoens when I had to kill a rat in my room my first night in New Delhi.

It didn't seem like an auspicious start. I'd seen rats during two previous visits to India, but in far worse rooms, which was why this rat was such a surprise. This particular room, in Paharganj, New Delhi's Main Bazaar, actually had a window. At three dollars a night it was a deal. I loved deals. That was one reason I liked India: it was such a bargain. When I'd arrived, the manager had flung his arms wide in welcome as if I was a long-lost brother. The gesture caused his bare belly and breasts to jiggle obscenely. But he was a jolly sort and admirably unself-conscious about the fact that he needed a brassiere or that his so-called office doubled as the hotel dumpster. There were dirty plates, rags, chairs, newspapers, a studded snow tire. He took a seat behind a battered desk and then informed me of the joyous news: the deposit was only four hundred rupees, or, as he put it, "Rupees four hundred." In 1989, four hundred rupees was about forty bucks U.S.

"Forty-dollar deposit for a three-dollar room?"

"Yes."

"That's crazy."

He smiled jubilantly. "Yes, crazy."

"I'm not paying four hundred rupees."

"Three hundred."

"No."

"Two hundred."

I picked up my pack to leave, despite the fact that it was eleven at night and I was exhausted. I'd just flown Vancouver — Singapore — Delhi.

"Okay-okay." He didn't appear troubled.

Before handing over any money, however, I scrutinized the room. The light worked. That was a good sign. I sniffed the bed. Clean. I checked under the pillow. No bugs. I pulled back the cover. No hairs, no stains, no imprint of a body. I looked around. There was even a desk, a chair, and a coat hanger. The coat hanger would come in handy.

"Great."

I paid him, got the key, then went in and locked the door. So, here I was back in India for the third time. I felt relief. I felt the satisfaction of the escapist. I laughed silently — I'd got away! It didn't matter that I hadn't been pursued. What mattered was that, divorced and directionless, I'd got away from Vancouver, a place that reminded me of the past.

Stepping from the arid air of the 747 earlier that evening, I'd recognized a welcome smell: *bidis*, hand-rolled Indian cigarettes, wrapped in a eucalyptus leaf and tied with cotton thread. They say smell is our most primal sense. The scent of *bidi* smoke was embedded deep in my brain as integral to India, the most pungent place I knew.

The airport's baggage belt was broken, so porters passed the luggage through by hand. The seeping walls were the colour of old egg yolk. A customs official picked his nose, stamped my passport, then picked his nose. Outside I recognized another smell — urine. Ignoring the taxi drivers, I headed for the Ex-Servicemen's Air Link Transport Service, the cheapest way into town. As I waited, it struck me that the descent from 35,000 feet did not end when the plane touched the tarmac but continued on to the bus, to the grubby part of the city, to the rock-bottom room. Now, standing in that room, I finally landed.

❄

Later that night, I woke to something probing my hair. I brushed at it and rolled over. It happened again. Then a third time. I turned on the light and studied the ceiling. Roach? Spider? Mosquito? For some reason, I squatted and looked under the bed. A rat. It was about a foot long, with the tail a foot and a half. It knew it'd been nabbed. I could tell by the look in its eyes. I grabbed the coat hanger and chased the rat as it darted into the bathroom. Cornered, it dashed side to side under the sink. A black, snub-nosed rat with a bald tail. It tried getting down the drain but couldn't fit. I gripped the coat hanger — a sturdy wooden job — and raised my arm. One whack was enough. It lay there, dead eyes staring like two beads of blood. I shovelled the corpse down the toilet hole in the floor, filled the bucket with water, and flushed it down. Then I sat on the bed, thinking of the rat scurrying along the headboard and nibbling my hair, thinking of plague, thinking also of the fact that I had come to India by choice. This was an experience I'd paid for. I reminded myself that I was here to visit the ex-Portuguese colonies of Goa, Daman, and Diu.

Staying in three-dollar rooms, I could stretch my stay out to a few months and avoid the Canadian winter, even if the Vancouver rain did not qualify as what is normally thought of as a Canadian winter. But the fact was, even if I had money, I'm such a penny pincher I couldn't enjoy an expensive room. The cost would torment me. So I'd be staying in cheapos anyway. Still, I didn't want to deal with any more rats, so that first night in New Delhi I made a resolution: by inching my standards up to four-dollar rooms, I could avoid vermin, stay a couple of months, learn about the Portuguese in India, and preserve my pecuniary peace of mind. But here I should make a point — the source of my cheapness is not a love of money per se but the time away from home it pays for, the time on the road it buys, the escape it permits.

I showered, packed, then stepped into the lobby. The manager was on his back on his desk, snoring loudly, one arm flung across his face, the other laid lovingly across his groin.

In the predawn light, New Delhi's Main Bazaar resembled the remnants of a carnival: hay, peelings, bottles, cow dung, and dead rats — suddenly they were everywhere. An old woman scraped muck with two boards and then slopped it into her cart. She was tiny and frail, and it was hard to imagine a sadder exercise in futility. Up the street, a shopkeeper opened his door, reached out, and poured a pot of filth. Splat. There. No longer his problem.

✳

"That's the problem with this damn place," said Ram. He was at the next table in the Madras Coffee House, where I'd sought refuge. "No one takes any responsibility for anything beyond their doorstep." Ram was an engineer who'd lived ten years in New York. He was about fifty, had smallpox scars on his face, and reminded me of the Indian actor Om Puri. I'd told him about the man and the garbage. Then I told him about the rat. He smiled grimly. "Yes. India is the land of plenty: plenty of poverty, plenty of people, plenty of rats."

"Why did you come back?" I asked him.

"You've been to New York?"

"No."

"I prefer Indian violence to American violence."

I didn't understand.

"In New York some bugger will come at you out of the blue. Boom. Cosh you on the nut. And not to rob you, either. But for kicks. In India that doesn't happen. Never. You can walk the streets at night no problem. Here it's crowds you have to worry about. Indians go mad in crowds. Something happens. I don't know. A kind of mania. That's why we can't hold elections without people being killed. That's why we can't hold demonstrations without people being killed. In the West you can do these things. But individually you are — " Ram put his finger to his temple and gave a twist. "Psycho." Then he asked, "What about you? Why are you here? Another bloody yuppie seeking a guru?"

I said I was on my way to the island of Diu, the smallest of Portugal's last three territories. From Diu the Portuguese had controlled access to the Gulf of Cambay, from which India's textiles had been shipped. I was excited by the fact that no one seemed to go there. Diu had been forgotten.

"Ah, yes," said Ram. "The Portuguese. A grubby bunch."

"But great sailors."

"Pirates."

He had a point. Yet it would be more accurate to say that the sixteenth-century Portuguese ran a seagoing protection racket. Their superior seamanship gave them total control of the Arabian Sea. Any ship caught without a pass, or *cartaz*, was fined or confiscated, often bloodily.

"It was a different era."

"Are you Portuguese?"

"No."

"You're just interested."

"They were the first to sail around Africa."

But Ram was immune to the mystique of the sea. "We had a Goan housekeeper," he said. "Teresa. Had a cross tattooed on her arm."

I mentioned Camoens. "He lived in Goa for eleven years in the sixteenth century."

Ram gazed at me with dark, droll eyes. "He has my sympathy."

To me eleven years in India seemed like an enormous achievement, especially since I'd never managed more than three months at one stretch. But Camoens was tough, a Renaissance man fluent with both the sword and the pen. He was a contemporary of Shakespeare. His *The Lusiads* is the most famous poem in Portuguese history. He fascinated me.

When Ram was gone, I looked around the dimly lit coffee-house, suspecting there were probably rats here too. I recalled the rats I'd seen in Morocco, badger-sized beasts haunting the tunnel-like alleys of the *souk* in Fez. I thought of rats I'd seen in Fiji, the "Little India of the South Pacific." I glanced under the table. Rat lore infested my mind. There was a rat temple somewhere in southern India, where the priests fed them each day. I'd read an article estimating that in Bombay there was a ratio of one rat to every person. Delhi, cleaner and inland, had a ratio of merely one rat for every two people. And then there was the night, on my last trip, in the Old Delhi Railway Station, where I watched hundreds of rats gush like oil from around the base of a pillar. They poured along the tracks and streamed across the rafters. One even crossed the foot of an old woman squatting on the platform heating milk on a burner. To the Indians, rats seemed as insignificant as sparrows. To me, it was like being stuck in a Hitchcock film. And yet, even as I watched the rats, it struck me that there was something human in the way they moved. They were urban creatures, living relentlessly hectic lives. They populated a city unto themselves, a ratropolis, a rodent Delhi.

❀

The sunlight stabbed my eyes when I emerged from the Madras Coffee House. I stood with one hand shading my brow and watched Connaught Circus, a series of concentric roundabouts locked in a perpetual log-jam of cars, carts, cows, camels, and jeepneys. Circus was the right word.

Delhi is made up of New Delhi and Old Delhi. Old Delhi was also called the Walled City or Shahjahanabad. Shah Jahan is a Moghul emperor who moved his capital from Agra and completed a new one in Delhi in 1648. He wasn't the first to build on the site but the seventh, the first city dating back to the tenth century BC. New Delhi, built by the British in 1911, was the city's eighth incarnation, and Connaught Circus was its centre. V.S. Naipaul considered New Delhi "a disaster, a mock-imperial joke, neither British nor Indian, a city built for parades rather than people, and today given a correctly grotesque scale by the noisy little scooter-rickshaws that scurry about its long avenues and endless roundabouts." It may not have been built for people, but it was certainly occupied by them, about ten million.

I headed up Janpath past an army of Sikh taxi drivers assembled in an order only they understood. The upper stories of the shops and offices overhung the sidewalk, creating a shaded corridor where peddlers sold pens, birds, scissors, locks; offered to shine your sandals, read your palm, measure your blood pressure. An immensely fat fellow sat squeezed into a school desk, selling city maps.

"How long you have been in Delhi?" he enquired.

"One night. And you?"

He put his hand to his heart and inclined his head apologetically. "Just fifty-six years."

"Where were you born?"

"Oh, very south!"

I plodded up four flights to another hotel. It was run by two brothers, who assured me there were no rats in the rooms. My room did have, however, thirteen light switches, one of which was on the ceiling, though there was only one light.

❈

That afternoon I went to buy a train ticket. Like Calcutta and Madras, New Delhi has a foreigners-only booking office. The privilege made me feel guilty, but not guilty enough to wait in the long lines the Indians have to put up with. The travellers in the booking office were in their twenties, costumed in rags and vests and all manner of ethno-wear, doing *Midnight Express* on American Express. The only exotic among them was an elderly British gent who was sweating heavily in a dark blue suit.

"That doesn't look very comfortable," I said.

He said it was part of "The business."

"The business? What business is that?"

He mumbled, then admitted he sold "Defence products."

"Defence products?"

He declined to expand.

I prodded.

"They play games with us, and we play games with them."

I was intrigued. "And who wins?"

"The game never ends."

"Is game playing something the British taught India?"

"Well, it goes both ways, doesn't it? They taught us polo, and we taught them cricket."

He was on his way to Hyderabad. I asked about the famed Nizam, the richest man in the world in the 1940s.

"Ah, yes," he said, as if remembering him fondly. "Too much money by half. They say some gem merchant once tried selling him an opal the size of an egg. The Nizam admitted it was very pretty. If they could find a half dozen more, he could make buttons."

I steered him onto the subject of the Portuguese.

He said, "The Nizam wanted to buy Goa's harbour, Marmagao. He wanted a port. It was the only way Hyderabad could become an independent country once the British left."

"He didn't want to be part of India?"

"The thought horrified him."

"What did the British think?"

"Weren't having any of it, were we. No, Goa and the Portuguese were always an issue. We knew something would have to be done once we pulled out. The view was that Goa," and here he searched for the correct word, "was liable to the wrong influences if left unattached."

"Communism."

"Influences. Of course, we should have sent them packing ages ago. We did take over for awhile in 1800. Only withdrew out of politesse. Same with the French in 1808. I suppose," he mused, "we both felt sorry for them."

"For the Portuguese?"

"Always seem to need a bit of a bath."

I felt a little indignant. Only later, after leaving the ticket office, did I realize that I should have responded with the Portuguese poet Fernando Pessoa's observation that "The British discovered the sea only after being told where it was."

❉

I returned to the Madras Coffee House. While eating a bowel-burning curry, I thought of my route, which was to reach Diu via Jaipur, Udaipur, then Ahmadabad, and from there I didn't know, just keep heading south. After that, I'd continue on to Daman, Bombay, and then Goa.

Camoens reached Goa in September 1553, after "six evil months of my life at sea." The arrival of ships from "the Kingdom" was an event that brought everyone to the waterfront. Stores were closed and business suspended. The population of the city of Goa included Arabs, Chinese, Gujaratis, Malays, Armenians, half-castes, and African slaves. The crowd called the penniless soldiers and sailors *descamisados* ("men without shirts"), abused them mercilessly, and swindled them. Camoens probably spent his first few nights in one of Goa's licensed gambling houses, which rented out rooms. Although he'd arrived at the end of the rainy season, when the mosquito-breeding puddles were drying up and the skies clearing, I suspect Goa's palm-fringed shores and brilliant beaches were anything but paradise to him. He must have been feeling badly treated by fate, or God, or whatever it was a sixteenth-century Portuguese believed in. He'd fallen from courtier to castaway, and worse he'd lost Catherine de Ataide.

Camoens first saw her on Good Friday 1544, in the Church of the Chagas, "the Church of the Wounds." There, in the candlelight and incense, the blonde Catherine must have appeared angelic. As Beatrice was to Dante, so Catherine was to Camoens. She was fourteen, Camoens twenty. He managed a formal introduction and gave her some of his poems. They became entranced with each other. It was an idealized love that would never be physically consummated.

During this time, Camoens was also making a name for himself as a poet at the court of King John. He was meeting influential men and women. But Catherine de Ataide's father was struggling financially, so he intended his daughter to make a profitable marriage, which categorically excluded Luis de Camoens. The fact that the young man proceeded to write a play inadvertently insulting the king and queen — causing his exile from Lisbon — was convenient as far as Catherine's father was concerned. This exile in a small northern town was followed by two years in North Africa, defending Ceuta, where Camoens lost the sight in his right eye. When he returned to Lisbon, he found the court a closed door. His disgrace made him persona non grata, his disfigurement earned him ridicule, and his poverty reduced him to working as a copyist. This was his state when, drunk and miserable one night, he stabbed Gonçalo Borges and got himself thrown in prison and then exiled once again, this time to India.

✻

After a few days in Delhi, I took the night train to Jaipur, and at five in the morning I stood shivering outside the Jaipur station, watching a line of ghostly camels plod past. Loaded with sacks, they resembled a caravan that could have been a thousand years old, travelling by night along its ancient route. The coats of the camels were shaved in geometric designs, and the men leading them went barefoot and bundled in scarves. Overhead, stars glinted like bits of broken ice. Right in front of me, meanwhile, hissing touts insisted on their services. "Hotel? Taxi? Come, sahib, here, this way! Change money? Rickshaw?" A gang of rag-wrapped men pedalling bicycle rickshaws had gathered to meet the train, and one by one they pushed slowly off through the dark streets with their fares. The air smelled rather pleasantly of cold dirt and *bidi* smoke.

Within an hour I stood on a hotel roof, watching the sun unearth itself from the horizon and push through the ochre haze. I recognized something, which is that the early morning in India had always struck me, even in the cities, as a spiritual time, though maybe it was only the calm, the birds, and the scent of woodsmoke. Jaipur was called the Pink City because of the sandstone used in its original construction, yet smog had turned it into the Brown City.

My room had silver wallpaper with red velvet designs, a TV that didn't work, and five mirrors, one of which was on the ceiling. Forgotten cigarettes had burned black grooves into the side tables. After doing a thorough search for any signs of rats, I tried to sleep but kept thinking of the Portuguese. What intrigued me about them was their fall from a brief position of power to a long decline into utter obscurity. Their territories came to epitomize colonial decay. The Portuguese quality *saudade* — "melancholy" — reflected this faded glory. Something about this captivated me. They were great, then lapsed. I imagined old men, their uniforms chewed by mice and time, their minds yellowed by malaria and opium, recalling an era of fabled grandeur. In the case of the excommunicated Camoens, he endured years of bad luck and melancholy in Goa. He was poor, he was often in trouble, and his writing was unknown.

Leaving the hotel that afternoon, I discovered it had a uniformed doorman. What a difference jumping from a three-dollar room to a four-dollar room made. A few metres from the doorman lay a dead dog, bald body bloating softly in the sun. The dog appeared to have been there for days, apparently of no concern to the doorman, the locals, or public health officials, if such people existed. I bused to a Mughal palace built on a nearby hilltop. Its windows, screened by ornate stone fretwork, offered views of hills as bare and grey as elephant hide. This was desert, the sun hot, the shadows chilly, the wind dusty and relentless. Gazing out at the land, I tried imagining Diu and the ocean, 800 kilometres southwest, at the tip of Gujarat.

On the bus back into Jaipur, there was a warning stencilled onto the back of a seat:

> *Look Undeer [sic] Your Seat!*
> *There Could Be A Bomb!*
> *Raise Alarm!*
> *Earn Reward!*

But the only danger in Jaipur came from the gem merchants who shouted from doorways, and followed me along the sidewalk, corralling me and thrusting their cards into my hand.

> *Patel Brothers: Gemologists*
> *Call Day or Night*

One man introduced himself as Sonny Singh. He wore a white shirt and grey slacks, had a sharp, cleanly shaven face, and short hair brushed straight back. He spoke with a quiet confidence, as if there could be no thought of my refusing.

"Come."

"Where?"

His head jerked back in shock, as if I'd taken a swing at him. "My shop."

"I don't want any gems."

He understood this Western delusion. He was here to help. He inclined his head reassuringly. "Looking only."

"No."

"Looking is free."

"I don't want to look."

"You are not liking gems? What kind of man is not liking gems?"

"I'm hungry. I'm going to eat now."

This satisfied him. He smiled. He was about thirty, slender, and fine-boned. "After eating you will look."

I ducked into a restaurant and hid at a corner table. At the counter some enraged Israelis were refusing to pay full price for their tomato omelettes — or "tamatoe amolotte" as it was written in the menu — because there was no tomato. Gems meant nothing to me, and the idea of actually paying for them was absurd. Yet Sonny Singh was a determined salesman. When I stepped back outside half an hour later, he was waiting.

"This way."

"I'm going that way."

"You promised."

"I didn't promise."

Now Sonny Singh looked crushed. His universe had collapsed. More than this, he was saddened by my lack of honour. "You are not man of your word."

"I didn't give you my word."

"You are dishonourable man."

I started walking.

He caught up. "Why you will not come?"

"I told you, I don't want any gems."

"Looking only!"

I halted. "Why do you want me to look if I have no intention of buying? Why waste your time on me?" Pleased with my logic, I smugly awaited his answer.

He put his hand on his chest. "Because I love my gems. And I want you to love them too."

❋

At dawn the next day, I set out from the hotel to catch a bus to Udaipur, three hundred kilometres to the south. Yet by the end of the day, I'd find myself in Jaisalmer, five hundred kilometres to the west, almost at the Pakistani border.

What happened?

After escaping from Sonny Singh the previous day, I'd gone to the Jaipur station to buy an advance ticket to Udaipur and met that most popular of Indian words: "Impossible!"

"You mean I can't get a ticket to Udaipur?"

"Yes!"

"Do you mean yes I can or yes I can't?"

"You can!"

"When?"

"Tomorrow."

"But not now?"

"No!"

"Why?"

"Because it is impossible!"

Jaisalmer

"But tomorrow it is possible?"

"Of course!"

So the next day I arrived at the station before sunrise and joined the pleasingly short queue. A bus pulled in, one headlight dead, the other blinking as the bus bounced over the speed bumps. Passengers staggered off knuckling their sleep-stuck eyes. Among them was a tall, attractive English woman in her forties. She stood apart, surveying the scene and smoking a *bidi* with the easy elegance inborn to the beautiful. She saw me in the ticket line and strode straight over.

"Are you going to Jaisalmer?"

"Udaipur."

She touched my arm with her pianist's fingers. "But you must go to Jaisalmer. It's gorgeous."

I'd read of it. "The Golden City."

Eyes round, she leaned toward me. "And it is."

"Golden?"

"Like this." She blew on the end of her *bidi*, making it glow. "That's the colour of the city walls at sunset." She became truly concerned. "Oh, but you really must go. Udaipur's nice, but," she shrugged, "it can't compare, not with that puddle of pea soup they call a lake. Are you interested in architecture?"

"Well. . . ."

"If you see Jaisalmer, you will be. The *havellis* — "

"*Havellis?*"

"Merchant houses." She closed her eyes. "Stunning. And the desert!"

"How long does it take to get out there?"

She made a face as if to ask, what was time? "Eight hours. Nine tops."

She saw I'd almost reached the wicket. "Well," she said. "Good luck." She strolled out of the station and stepped into a rickshaw.

Perhaps because I lack it, I've always envied spontaneity. Even though I'm cautious, however, my imagination often runs ahead like a giddy child. To be blunt, my imagination can fuck me up. There was the time, for instance, I flew to Japan with all kinds of visions of becoming a Zen man. I'd have a house in a bamboo grove, practise kendo, calligraphy, and meditation. I'd have a serene and seductive Japanese woman. It was all set. All I had to do was go there and take occupancy of this elaborately constructed fantasy. So I did. And hated it. There were no rooms in Kyoto, and Osaka — cold and polluted and expensive — stunk. On top of that, one night some friends and I got mugged by a group of junior *yakuzas* known as *chimpira*. I left a week later, betrayed by my own fantasy life.

But that was a whole eight years ago. Now I knew when to stay and when to leap. When I reached the ticket window, I said "Jaisalmer."

Despite the bus being a battered old Tata with planks for seats, I knew I'd made the right move, especially when, twenty minutes after buying the ticket, we pulled out and the sun began to rise, expanding the horizon and making the sky glow like a glazed ceramic dome. Behind us and to the right, it sent long shadows streaming from every rock, and it warmed the bus with welcome heat.

This was Rajastan, king land, and the people were Rajputs, lean, gaunt-cheeked, and sharp-nosed. The men, it seemed to me, all looked like Lee Van Cleef from the movie *The Good, the Bad, and the Ugly*. They wore brown suit coats and sported brilliant yellow turbans and gold hoop earrings or the smaller, flower-shaped Rajput ear stud. The sexes sat separately, but both tended the children. Three men on the bench in front of me passed an infant boy back and forth, popping orange segments into his mouth, entertaining him, bouncing him. Behind me were three women each with a child in her lap.

By nine in the morning, the sun's welcome heat was turning the bus to a tin can in a bonfire. The dust and *bidi* smoke thickened the exhaust fumes smouldering up through the floorboards. Eight hours the English woman had said. Three down, five to go. Squeezed between two men on a plank bench little more than a metre long, I tried to sleep, but that wasn't easy. Since I was unable to sleep, the old man dozing next to me became more aggravating, especially because his head kept lolling sideways and resting on my shoulder. Still, I tried to be accommodating. I diverted myself by trying to see beauty in the landscape of endless grey scrub. I thought of the Buddhists and all their meditative patience. It didn't help. Of course, I could have taken a luxury coach, but that would have cost me, oh, ten dollars, whereas the local bus was half that amount. I consoled myself with the money I was saving. Yet I was bored and tired, and, more than anything, I wanted the blissful oblivion of sleep. I shrugged the old man off. He straightened, blinked, then dozed again. The young guy to my right had also managed to doze, his head against the window.

Jaisalmer

GRANT BUDAY

What a skill they all possessed! What a secret! Even the three men in front of me fell asleep. The one in the middle was particularly maddening because his head rested on the bare bar that ran along the top of the seat. The bar vibrated so violently that his skull bounced with every rut we hit, but he slept soundly, dreaming his dreams. Jealous of his capacity for unconsciousness, I kicked the back of his seat. If I couldn't doze, then no one would. He raised his head, looked left, looked right, then dropped right off again.

I began to hate spontaneity.

❋

We reached Jodhpur at two in the afternoon. In eight hours I'd gone from fresh-faced enthusiasm to eye-twitching despair. I estimated we had seven more hours to go.

Leaving my bag and my bottle of water on the rack above the seat, I got off the bus to stretch my legs. Starving, I joined the others at a table where they were spooning up a red stew in which I recognized a jawbone and some vertebrae.

"What is it?"

"Goat."

I had nothing against goat. I'd eaten dog in Manila and, despite its stringy, vealish texture, had not only kept it down, but gone away satisfied. But there was something about those vertebrae, and that jawbone that still had teeth in it. I opted for a two-rupee packet of cookies.

Jodhpur's buildings had walls of blazing white, its streets were chalk dust, and the sun burned like an acetylene torch. I supposed that *jodhpurs* — "riding breeches" — were named after the town. I was too tired to care. Back on the bus, I discovered that my bottle of water was missing. In India, it's bottled water or diarrhoea or, worse, dysentery. Of course, some people claim they drink the water, but they're liars, just like guys who say they broke a hundred the first time they golfed. No one else was on board. I got back off the bus to find a stall where I could buy another bottle. At that point, though, the driver returned and honked the horn, and everyone ran to reboard. When I squeezed my way back into my seat, I discovered my bottle of water was back, exactly where I'd left it.

The young guy next to me smiled. "I drank it."

"It was mine."

"I refilled it."

"You refilled it?"

"Of course," he said, as if I was accusing him of theft.

"Where?"

"There." He pointed out the window to a pump, upon which a dog was peeing. Drinking water from that pump would have left me shitting blood.

"Thank you."

"You are welcome."

The bus pulled out. At least we were under way again. Sixty seconds later, however, we weren't under way, because the driver stopped the bus and vanished, and for the next hour we just sat there. What made it worse was that the Indians didn't seem concerned. They fell asleep. When the young guy next to me stirred briefly to change positions, I asked him why we'd halted.

He said, "I don't know," then closed his eyes.

At that point the only person other than me who was awake was a child behind me. She began groping my neck with slimy fingers. I turned and glared at her mother, but she too was sleeping, so I sat forward, put my head in my hands, and tried to be mature. It was a tough task. Camoens was six months on a foul and stinking ship, and I couldn't handle a day on a bus. I forced my way off and stood in the street. Then, as if condemned to some Buster Keaton farce, the bus started up, spewed smoke in my face, and began pulling away. I ran behind pounding the back. When it halted I got on and confronted the driver, who weighed about seventy-five pounds and had a goiter. Too weary and miserable to speak, I staggered to my seat and sat down. The old man to my left fell asleep again with his head on my shoulder.

Between kicking the seatback of the man sleeping in front of me — and then feeling like a rat when he later offered me an orange — the afternoon ground past. Eventually, I found myself at a rest stop, standing in the shade of a six-storey sand dune, sipping chai. The sun was almost down, and the dunes, sculpted to perfection by the winds, were all shades of pink and grey. The sky, cooling at last, had taken on a deep and restful blue. I felt an almost tearful relief. The heat had relented, the trip was nearly over, and the desert was a splendid place to be. I'd have stayed there forever, happy to sip chai with these patient people, watching the colours change and the sand swirl. We experienced the onset of evening as if it were as spectacular as an eclipse. Even a local man in a yellow turban, squatting under a tree across the road with his arm around a goat, seemed moved by the moment.

Jaisalmer

An hour later, however, that epiphany had been reduced to a remote memory. Four hours after that and still on the road, it had never happened. It was not until midnight that we reached the mountain that rose out of the Great Indian Desert and that twelfth-century builders had transformed into the city of Jaisalmer. The eight-hour trip had taken eighteen hours, but it was done, and in the darkness the looming outline of the medieval walls announced that the trip had been worth it. It even wiped out all thoughts of having to endure the same trip over again to get back on track to Diu. At the base of the hill, touts met the bus. We walked through the gate and up lanes paved with sandstone blocks, into the walled city with its carved and overhanging balconies silhouetted by starlight. The place smelled of cool stone. I was led to a hotel outside of which dogs howled all night.

❋

In the morning, I opened the door to find five men seated before it playing cards. As I edged past they acknowledged me by inclining their heads with great solemnity. It turned out that they were the manager's uncles, and they sat there from sunrise to sunset every day, playing cards, sipping chai, and talking. I walked across the courtyard and sat on a plastic chair in the sun. As I was sitting there, a one-armed German strode over and presented his foot for me to tie his shoelace. How did I know he was German? I suppose it was the blond hair, the Aryan cheekbones, something in his manner. One of his shirt sleeves hung as limp as a windsock. I thought of the actor Klaus Maria Brandauer. As I tied his shoelace, I suggested he buy a pair of slip-ons. He said nothing, just nodded and then strolled out through the stone gate. I didn't see him again until that evening, at sunset, when I spotted him juggling three stones on the hotel roof. He'd positioned himself so that his shadow fell full on a brick wall that glowed, just as the English woman had said, like coals.

She had also been right about the *havellis*, the houses of merchant families, who had grown rich on the trade of caravans from Damascus. They evoked an *Arabian Nights* charm and hinted of erotic intrigues unfolding behind the fabulously detailed grilles and windows. The English woman and I were not the only ones impressed by the architecture. Here is what one Indian guidebook has to say:

> *The havellis of Patwa, Salim Singh, Diwan Nathmal and Chiriya are high imposing.*
>
> *Massive gateways, open courtyards and narrow lanes give Jaisalmer its majestic atmospheres. Houses that are high, cluster in close rows along the cobbled street. Domes, pillars, arches, walls, balconies almost everything is carved out geometrically and ornamented with floral and representational patterns that have animal, bird and human figures.*
>
> *The most exquisite and unique architectural features of these structures are the sterabotic ground floor columns, symmetrical friezes supported by brackets and hosses; projecting balconies, kiosk platforms having covette mouldings ridges of roofs having either crenellated parapets crowned with balustrades.*

GRANT BUDAY

The knotted syntax reflected the overwrought rococo of the
havellis. Too bad Jaisalmer's finest corners and lanes were
also used as toilets. In a curious reversal the people did it out-
doors and the mice indoors. Each morning I found fresh
mouse turds on my toilet seat. But the room cost only three
and a half dollars, and, in the Hierarchy of Vermin, mice were
preferable to rats. The Hierarchy of Vermin was something I'd
invented after years of experience in lousy rooms throughout
Asia. Snakes topped the list even though I'd never met one.
They were followed by rats, then lice, then mice, and then
mosquitoes. After them came bedbugs, then cockroaches,
which, admittedly disgusting, are at least harmless. Finally,
there were geckos, those putty-pale lizards that cling to walls
and ceilings and are, in fact, considered good luck.

Were I freer with my money, the Hierarchy of Vermin
would never have been devised. But what could I do? Being
obsessively cheap is somewhat analogous to my being left-
handed: I could change, but it would be just too much work
and would never feel quite natural.

I lingered for a week in Jaisalmer. One afternoon near the
end of that week, I watched a family of itinerant blacksmiths
who'd set themselves up outside the city walls. They'd built a
fire and laid out their tools. The young wife swung the sledge-
hammer, her bangles sliding along her ropey forearms, her
yellow head cloth clenched in place with her teeth. Her
husband had the easy job, squatting by a fire and puffing a
bidi while gripping a pair of tongs. He heated a rod until the
tip glowed pink, then using pliers he twisted the tip into a
loop, which he then held on the anvil while she hammered

34

the loop until it merged into a solid surface and eventually became a spoon.

I also visited the residence of a British colonial administrator that had been turned into a museum. The house in itself was not remarkable, the dark furniture embedded with decades of dirt, the rugs reduced to cords. But what was remarkable was the atmosphere of spirit-stifling loneliness. I sat a long time in one of the chairs with its wide wooden arms, listening to the wind off the desert, its hypnotic voice making me feel so forlorn that I began to understand why some people fear wind. I studied the old photographs. Group portraits of resplendent Rajastani nobles, turbaned, bearded, silked, their swords in gem-studded scabbards. Yet in each case my attention went to the solitary Englishman in the picture: tight suit, lacquered hair, shaved face. The odd man out. The emblem of reserve. One in particular held my eye, an Englishman in a chair, perhaps the very chair I'd been sitting in. He gazed straight out at the camera, face set, rigidly holding the pose, the model of decorum. The handwritten date said 1922. Sixty-seven years ago. The man looked like he was in his twenties. He could still be alive, but I doubted it, not because of the years but because he looked condemned and his eyes were screaming — dark and still, but screaming. He looked like a suicide photographed minutes before the act.

❀

The manager of the hotel I was staying in was named Daulat. He was about thirty, had the hard, handsome look of a movie sheik, and exhibited the eerie calm of a man who possessed absolute conviction in a cause. Each day he came into my room and took a chair, seating himself with the easy grace of an athlete and then questioning me. What is your education? What is your job? How much do you earn? Do you own a house? A car? Are you married? Why not? Daulat was unfailingly gracious, but I had the feeling that I was permitted to live only because of his mood.

The day I told Daulat I would be leaving and heading for Diu, he insisted I take the bus.

"The train will be more comfortable," I said. It had been a wonderful discovery to find that there was a train station here in Jaisalmer.

"No," said Daulat. "Bus is comfortable. And faster. You must take bus."

"I took the bus out here. It wasn't comfortable, and it wasn't fast."

"You must take first-class bus."

"But why?"

"It is best." To Daulat, apparently, there could be no more incontrovertible reason than this.

"But why is it best?"

"Because it is." He had large, heavy-lidded eyes that gazed at me with dark, direct certainty. He said he was going to Delhi next week. By bus. When I asked about his business in the capital, he would only say, "For political purposes."

Political purposes? That worried me. What was he up to? Was there going to be a bomb on the train? Was he warning me? I considered following his advice. Yet when I recalled the bus ride out from Jaipur, I decided to risk the bomb and take the train.

✻

Since the train line began — or ended depending on which way you were going — at Jaisalmer, I had the rare opportunity of boarding an Indian train that was empty. The first few hours en route to Udaipur, I actually had a compartment to myself. By Jodhpur that had changed. By the time we reached Udaipur, it was so crowded I couldn't raise my arms, much less reach the lavatory.

I stayed just one night in Udaipur before continuing on to Ahmadabad. Udaipur is a small city surrounded by small mountains, with an island palace in a lake whose weedy water is, as that English woman had said, as thick and green as pea soup. Along the shore, men and women beat their laundry against rocks, like so many victims in a Greek myth condemned to perform the futile task of breaking stones with hammers of cloth. Their chances of getting their clothes clean in such murk were just as likely.

I visited one of the islands in the lake. The narrow boat that ferried me out parted the weedy purée that took the place of water. I wandered between families picnicking on the flat grassy island.

"Sheila! Take that out of your nose!"

"Noor! Stop that or I'll set you on fire!"

"You bugger, I'll slap you silly!"

In the evening, I went to the Lake Palace Hotel, and, just to prove what a rollicking spendthrift I could be, I blew four and a half dollars on a single bottle of Kingfisher beer, an indulgence that I made last for over an hour. The hotel's architecture showed Mughal influence. Before the sun dropped behind the hills, it sent slanting rays through the strategically placed windows, filling the tiled halls with cinnamon-coloured light.

✵

The night bus from Udaipur got me into Ahmadabad the following morning. I immediately bought an onward train ticket for that night and then, practicalities taken care of, took a look around. Ahmadabad was called the City of Dust, and for good reason. Dust silted the streets, lay thick over every surface, and was gusted by everything that moved. The streets appeared to be filled with smoke. Cyclists and rickshaw wallahs wore bandanas across their faces, making Ahmadabad resemble a City of Bandits.

To pass the time, I got a haircut. The barber wore glasses so scratched it looked like he'd been cleaning the lenses with sixty-grit sandpaper. Three other barbers watched me from behind identical lenses. Only the positions of their heads indicated the direction of their gaze. Still, I leaned back in the chair and submitted to the quick snick-snick-snick of the bird-beak scissors and listened to the flutey chatter. It was a relief not understanding the language. All I heard was its sound. When the barber eventually finished, I moved to get up, but his hand pressed me back down. He took my head in a wrestling hold and began knuckling one side of my skull. Then he changed arms and knuckled the other side. When this was done, I laughed with embarrassed relief and started getting up — again his hand pressed me back down. He rubbed scented oil between his palms and then proceeded to slap me about the head with a rough professional ease. As he yanked and tugged my hair, I felt my face pulled and stretched like a rubber mask. When this was finally over, I jumped up, sheet around my neck. He stalked me with a shaving brush full of lather, indicating my unshaven neck below my beard. I sighed and sat back down. When at last I was permitted to leave, having shaken hands with all four barbers and their customers, I stepped into the street with my head floating and my scalp singing.

Within half an hour, however, the City of Dust had drained me. I considered getting a hotel room and sleeping. I even walked past a few and sized them up. Unable to part with the cash, I opted for a park bench, beneath which rats rustled in the fallen leaves. I dozed and thought ahead to Diu. Many of the older people there would likely speak Portuguese, have Portuguese names, and be Roman Catholic. I recalled Joseph Conrad's novel *An Outcast of the Islands*, which includes a disparaging though intriguing reference to the da Souzas.

That family's admiration was the great luxury of his [Willems's] life. It rounded and completed his existence in a perpetual assurance of unquestionable superiority. He loved to breathe the coarse incense they offered before the shrine of the successful white man; the man that had done them the honour to marry their daughter. . . . He fed and clothed that shabby multitude; those degenerate descendants of Portuguese conquerors; he was their providence; he kept them singing his praises in the midst of their laziness, of their dirt, of their immense and hopeless squalor: and he was greatly delighted.

Willems did not interest me so much as the da Souzas. That they represented lassitude and popish superstition only added to their charm. Give me more bamboo crucifixes, give me more churches decaying dangerously toward idolatrous jungle temples. I felt the same attraction during my stay in Portugal ten years before, where I found the people a sad and quirky lot. And there was even my landlord in Vancouver, Manuel. I lived in an old house broken up into suites. Manuel, short, dark-skinned, ingenuous, talked loudly to himself in Portuguese, kept his pants up with a length of baling twine, fixed broken doorknobs with Scotch tape, and made wine in oak casks. He'd spent eight years in Angola, had a grade three education, yet owned two large houses and a number of cars and took a month-long holiday to Cuba each winter. He also had a colourful image of Fatima dangling from the rearview mirror of his VW Rabbit.

Before leaving Vancouver, I'd asked him, "Do you know anything about the Portuguese in India, Manuel?"

"Oh, India." He'd shaded his eyes and gazed down the alley as if he might see it in the distance. "In olden day Por-too-gal very strong." He'd made a fist. "But now?" He'd shrugged and given me a baleful look. Then he'd resumed talking to the lawn mower.

I'd been reading about Renaissance Portugal and found it helpful to put 1498, the year Vasco da Gama reached India, in perspective by orienting it in relation to other events. Just six years earlier, for example, in 1492, Columbus reached the New World. Also in 1492, Granada, the last Muslim city in Spain, fell to the Catholic forces. In 1498, da Vinci had just finished painting *The Last Supper*. In 1500, a Portuguese squadron sailing west to find the trade winds would accidentally discover Brazil. It would be twenty-two more years before Magellan, another Portuguese, circumambulated the Earth in 1522 and another nineteen before Mercator built his first globe in 1541.

In 1553, Camoens reached Goa. He was not there a month before he joined a flotilla of thirty-five ships and twelve hundred men and sailed to the Red Sea in pursuit of the Turkish fleet. There he saw the method of the Portuguese in the East, which was to butcher everyone aboard an enemy ship, even those who wanted to surrender. For Camoens, this tarnished the myth of the sterling Portuguese and the heroic achievements of glorious Lusitania. Back in Goa, faced yet again with his lack of money, Camoens began supplementing his soldier's pay by writing letters for the illiterate. In sixteenth-century Goa, that meant most everyone. Camoens had studied at Coimbra, Portugal's most famous university, yet now at the age of thirty-one he was reduced not only to writing letters for others but also occasionally to accepting chickens in lieu of cash.

❊

Although I only had a second-class ticket, I'd slipped into the first-class waiting room of the Ahmadabad station and now sat waiting for my train south to Sior. As I waited, I watched a Sikh perform his toilet. He stood before a bench taken up entirely by his open suitcase, his clothes, and an array of tubes, combs, and surgical-looking instruments. He twisted his hair into a rope and hooked it up under his chin. He bound his jaw in a black cloth that he knotted atop his head as if he had a toothache. Then he wrapped a white cloth across his mouth and tied it at the back of his neck as if he were a bandit. Trussed and smothered, he disappeared into the washroom. He emerged a minute later and sprayed his armpits, untied the cloths from his head, took up a turban, and rewrapped his head, taking three tries before getting it right. This looked painful. Standing before the mirror, he took a long metal pin and prodded his hair up under his turban. He turned his head side to side, inspecting himself. Satisfied, he dropped his pants. The length of his shirt assured his modesty. He pulled on a fresh pair of trousers, packed up his equipment, exchanged rubber thongs for leather sandals, and, swaddled and wrapped, departed looking extremely uncomfortable.

At midnight I found my compartment and the two people I'd be sharing it with: the Meehan sisters.

"We were wondering what you'd look like. Thought you were going to miss the train. We're on a fortnight's visit from Glasgow, it's so cold and damp there now. We saw Diu on the map, and I said look at that wee island way down there, I doubt anyone ever goes it's so far, so we said right, we'll do it. Three straight days from Delhi, we're knackered." Short, thirtyish, red-haired, freckled, identical, they gazed at me. "We went to Borneo last year, and this time we're prepared. We've brought plenty of bog paper." Marilyn, the more talkative, unzipped a satchel and showed me a supply of toilet paper that would last not just two weeks but two years.

"You can buy toilet paper here."

"Well, our book says they use their fingers," said Marilyn.

"I'm game for anything," put in Marie, "but there's a limit. I'll ruin me nails."

The Meehans worked in the hotel business. It also turned out that they liked to drink. They had two bottles of Indian gin nestled safely among those toilet rolls, and they existed in a state of perpetual wonder at finding India different from Scotland, especially in matters of alcohol.

"Took us all day to get the permit to buy this gin." They produced cups and limes and soda and poured a round as we waited for the train to pull out.

❋

At 3 a.m., the Meehans and I got off the train at Sior, where we had to find a jeepney to Palitana, from where a bus would hopefully get us to Diu. We were drunk. The train chugged off, and we were left amid the hiss of the cicadas. We looked around. The Sior station was a slab of cement and a bench. That wasn't odd, but there were no touts, and that was odd. We looked at each other. Someone had to go off and find a jeepney.

I left the Meehans with the packs and wandered down a street. As my eyes adjusted to the dark, I discovered the street aswirl with, what else, rats. They flowed as thick as mud. I recalled a Danish girl in Colombo who got bit on the foot by a rat and endured a series of thirteen rabies shots through the navel. I turned around, feeling especially vulnerable in my sandals. I was jogging back toward the station when a single headlight overtook me. I leapt about like a castaway signalling a ship. The jeepney picked me up, and a minute later we swung in alongside the platform, making a mighty impression upon the ladies. I was a hero. Ten minutes after that, we glided out of Sior and into the hills under the stars. The driver was wrapped in towels; the Meehans and I shared a blanket and the gin. We settled back.

India. Exactly where I wanted to be. What a rare moment — I was perfectly satisfied with life.

Twenty-five kilometres from Palitana, the jeepney died. The driver poked a stick into the gas tank. Dry. The Meehans opened the other bottle of gin. I suggested pouring some into the tank, but the driver placed his body between me and the vehicle, though he gladly took a swig. His name was Mohun. We all laughed. Mohun and the Meehans. Eventually, a truck appeared — growing bigger and brighter as it barrelled toward us — then smaller and dimmer as it travelled right on by. Half an hour later, a bus swung into view. I stood the Meehans in the road and shone the flashlight on them. The bus halted, I paid off Mohun and shook his hand, and we climbed on. As the bus picked up speed, so did my imagination.

What, for example, happened when the Portuguese ships ran out of wind? If the sails sagged and the sea turned to glass, what then? Drift? Watch and wait? I had some firsthand experience in the matter, having once sailed from Fiji to New Zealand on a twenty-four metre ketch. The boat had been built in 1896 and was rigged only with block and tackle. There were no power winches anywhere. In the middle of the crossing, we were becalmed for four days. While some of my shipmates found it bemusing to be adrift, with the boat rolling from rail to rail and the crockery shattering, I was terrified. Not because I feared we'd sink, but because I felt trapped.

Others felt they shared the freedom of a ship at sea; I saw only that small deck, a cabin full of cockroaches, and the fact that I couldn't escape. We had a motor, of course, but the captain, a salty Swede who'd been around the world three times, was not about to waste precious fuel just because the wind was taking a little vacation. So there we wallowed. I was twenty and learning the hard lesson that I was not a sailor.

Camoens was. And he was tough. Still, he must have suffered during that hurricane off the African coast en route to India and on the days when he too was becalmed. People in those days must have had a different sense of time and a lot of patience. They must have felt like mice against the sea. And then, of course, there was the wind, the invisible wind that could carry them around Africa or onto the rocks or, fickle as an ornery god, abandon them. In the still and stifling air, each man's fears would rise, poisonous and tentacled, to the surface. Personalities would rub. A knife in the night would be as inevitable as worm in the biscuit.

❈

We reached Palitana as the sun rose. As it set, I vomited curry from the balcony of my hotel room. A dozen Gujaratis in an ox cart stopped to smoke *bidis* and take in the show. I amazed myself with how loudly I vomited and took some small solace in this capacity to be amazed, for it meant a stable corner remained in my mind. The sun set into the desert with a magnificent red indifference while I continued to retch. Then, lying exhausted on the bed, I heard the Meehans gabbling in Glaswegian in the next room. They'd eaten the same food I had but were chipper with health. All night I swallowed bottled water and then vomited it under the stars.

At sunrise the Meehans shoved me aboard a bus. By noon we had reached Maua, the ugliest town on Earth. Goats grazed the dirt lot of the bus station, eating paper and peelings. A plastic bag dangled half-shat from one goat's anus. Dogs circled and snarled, pigs snuffled the open sewer, buses pumped smoke, chickens pecked gobs of snot. No one behind the wire wicket could tell us which bus was heading for Diu, so we simply had to wait and be ready. When the Diu bus was finally announced, we rushed the door. The crowd carried me up and in, but the Meehans didn't make it, they were lost at the perimeter waving plaintively at me, so I fought my way off, and we watched the bus depart. It looked like a rootbound pot, legs and arms and heads sticking out of windows, people waving from the roof. The stationmaster admitted that the next bus, in three hours, would be "very worse." We wandered forlornly out of the station and met a man leaning against the hood of a taxi, arms crossed, as if he'd been watching our pathetic efforts. Ten minutes later we'd settled on eighteen dollars for the three of us and piled in.

The Meehans were soon asleep. The stony desert spread out to the horizon in all shades of ochre and tan, and my respect for the early travellers increased yet again. Camoens: seventeen years in Asia, no buses, no taxis, no flights or American Express, just ship and foot and patience. As much as the hardship, it was the patience that impressed me. An entire winter waiting for a caravan, a hurricane season waiting for safe sailing conditions. Under such restrictions, what could those venturers do but stop looking ahead and start looking around, at the trees, the temples, the coins, the clothes? Those Portuguese like Camoens who journeyed out to India must have known every inch of their ship, right down to the knots in the rails. Camoens would have seen the ropes oiled so they didn't dry and snap. He'd have seen the decks watered every evening so they didn't shrink and leak. He'd have known the complexion of each sail as well as the groans and aches of the ship's timbers. The sows would have given birth, and men would have died and been slid over the rail into the sea. In the 1500s, the voyage from Lisbon to India averaged six months, and on average fifty percent of the people aboard died.

On the other hand, not all travellers had it so rough. In my reading, I'd come across a Monsieur Jacquement of Calcutta, who — being French, after all — seemed to know how to tour India in style. In 1829, he wrote to a friend in the French colony of Pondicherry:

> I wake before daybreak in a tent . . . and call the roll, still from beneath my blankets, a job which is soon done, for I have only nine men to call over. Thereupon my head valet . . . enters with a lantern and a pot of water. In ten minutes' time I am dressed. . . . Thereupon a procession enters: first the cook, with a tumulus of rice beneath which are buried the component parts of a chicken; the syce, or groom, come to fetch my horse's saddle; the under-valet, who rolls up the blankets, folds the bed and shuts up my shaving apparatus; and another servant belonging to the hierarchy of Indian domesticity,

*who is oleaginous in his functions and has, among his
other duties, that of keeping my guns and pistols in good
order. While all this is going on inside the tent my chief
quartermaster, who presides over the tent, is at work outside demolishing it in such a way that, when everything
has been dragged out of it and all the men have come
out too, it falls as though by a magic spell, and is immediately rolled up, made in a bundle, and loaded on a
waggon, while I reduce my tumulus of pilau to a dead
level with my plate as I preside over the operations.*

✻

Even before we reached the sea we smelled the stink of fish
racks. They stood all along the shore, hung with fish sliced
paper-thin to dry in the sun. The salt wind gusted sand across
the trail of tarmac that ended at the remnants of a dock.
Across the narrow strait stood Diu.

The Meehans breathlessly discussed the possibility of por-
ridge while a converted fishing boat took us the 200 metres
across. Climbing the stone steps of the jetty, we were greeted
by alcohol advertisements painted on the walls. Johnson
Whiskey — "It's Great to Be High!" Sandpiper Whiskey —
"Roll Scotland on Your Tongue!" "Bullet Beer Goes up Like
a Shot!" "Drink Kingfisher!"

It was Friday afternoon, and the grog shops were over-
flowing with Gujaratis. Gujarat was dry, while Diu's premier
industry was distilling. The visiting drunks were already
staggering. In doorways, the locals seemed sadly resigned
to another sleepless weekend. The Portuguese blood was

immediately obvious in many of the older faces, as was the influence in the architecture, the tiled street names, and the coats-of-arms on old houses.

We got two rooms on the third floor of the Pensao del Mar, with balconies overlooking the strait. The Meehans immediately went in search of booze. I went to the fort, which took up one end of the island. My first impression was that Arthurian pennants could have flapped from its towers. Immense stone sides sloped back from the tidal moat, and cannons protruded from the crenellated walls. The main doors were built of massive planks and armoured with iron spikes. The fort had been built in 1546 and was now used as a jail.

A guard in a dirt-brown uniform said there were three prisoners. He pointed his rifle at a row of pigeon-hole windows high on an inner wall.

"Gold smugglers." He grinned. "Pakistani. Muslim." He seemed to savour this last detail. He gestured with his chin, and we listened to one prisoner singing the call to prayer, a forlorn voice quavering from within the stone.

"How long will they serve?"

"One years. Maybe five."

The majority of the fort was derelict. A parched garden in the central courtyard had pyramids of lopsided stone cannonballs. A metal statue of Vasco da Gama stood by one wall. In an empty room, I discovered an iron-grated hole in the floor: a cell. I hoped those Pakistani gold smugglers had cheerier quarters. From a guard tower, I looked out over the arid island at a hazy sea the colour and texture of hammered lead.

Back at the Pensao del Mar, the Meehans sat on the balcony drinking cashew fenny — which smelled like lighter fluid — and wondering about the likelihood of water skiing. I looked at the narrow strait below. In contrast to the grey of the open ocean, it was the colour of newly poured cement. A fishing boat chugged past. A man poled a skiff.

I retired early, but didn't sleep long because booze was doing dark things to the group of Gujaratis sharing the next room. One wept and then ran howling onto the balcony, where he tried flinging himself over. His friends wrestled him back inside. A few minutes later they all left. I went onto the balcony and watched them emerge from the hotel carrying the man in a rolled carpet, slide him onto the back seat of an Ambassador, and squeal off.

This scene brought to mind an observation made by Paul Bowles while he was travelling in Turkey in 1953. It appears in his book *Their Heads Are Green and Their Hands Are Blue.*

> *It is to be expected that there should be a close relationship between the culture of a given society and the means used by its members to achieve release and euphoria. For Judaism and Christianity the means has always been alcohol; for Islam it has been hashish. The first is dynamic in its effects, the other static. If a nation wishes, however mistakenly, to Westernize itself, first let it give up hashish.*

❀

The next afternoon I went into Saint Paul's Cathedral, built in 1601 of limestone and teak. The cooing of the pigeons nesting on the ledges added to the soothing ambience of the dark interior. A side door led to a courtyard, in the centre of which stood a dry fountain. Another door led to a dark room striped with slats of dusty sunlight. Life-sized carvings of saints and Christs and Virgins had been stored here. There was a hand-pulled funeral cart of black wood and chipped gold paint. Although a long-lapsed Catholic myself, I felt a certain relief amid the familiar in a foreign land. And if I felt it, surely those sixteenth-century Portuguese who arrived here felt it more, even if only wishing to escape the sun in favour of the cool interiors of the church. I imagined those Portuguese spending many afternoons within these shady walls.

The Portuguese cemetery sat in solitude amid the wind-whipped scrub. It was locked, though the rusted chain and rotted gate could easily have been forced open. I climbed onto the stone wall and read the names on the crooked crosses: Coutu, da Silva, Luis, Rodriguez, Mesquita. Behind me, the hazy sky went ochre with sunset, waves of black glass broke on the rocks, a crow cawed, and pigeons clattered. Pereira, Bosco, da Costa, Tome. All buried beneath the salt-parched dirt. It seemed a melancholy thing to die so far from home.

The next day I met Father Goes, the one priest remaining on Diu. He was thirty, smelled of coconut oil, and spoke a fluid English. His white silk soutane shone in the sun. He was writing a history of Diu.

"Indian nationalism is excellent! I am Indian. But I am also of Portuguese ancestry and a Catholic. Why must I forget this?" He gazed at me as if I had the answer. We stood inside Diu Fort. Taking me by the elbow, he guided me to the ten-foot statue of Vasco da Gama. "This is not da Gama. It is Nuno da Cunha, ninth viceroy of Portuguese India. The church, furthermore, is not Saint Paul's but Our Lady of the Immaculate Conception." He shook his head. "And if for nothing else the fort should be reconstructed as a tourist attraction. But let's face facts, the Indian government — my government — is so corrupt and inefficient they cannot even establish a sea link to Bombay, much less reopen the airport." Disheartened, he stared at the dirt. "History is a high price to pay for nationalism."

I wondered what Camoens would have thought about Father Goes's concerns. Or about the fact that some 400 years later a young man — me — from an as yet undiscovered coast, would contemplate him. And what indeed did the Indians think of those first Portuguese? One description goes like this: the Portuguese who first arrived at Calicut were a "race of very white and beautiful people, who wear boots and hats of iron and never stop in any place. They eat a sort of white stone and drink blood."

✻

Acquiring Diu was not easy for the Portuguese. They tried taking it in 1518 but were defeated by the Gujaratis. Another attempt in 1521 also failed. A fleet of three hundred ships, led by Nuno da Cunha in 1531, was foiled by a blockade of chains. Only by harassing and capturing Gujarati ships did the Portuguese finally force the sultan of Gujarat into signing a treaty in 1534 that permitted them to build a fort. In 1546, Governor Joao de Castro wanted to build a new and bigger fort. He had to pledge his beard for a loan from the Municipal

Council of Goa. The story goes that he even gave orders to have the bones of his son unearthed so that he could send them to Goa as proof of his reliability. Embarrassed, the council not only gave him the loan but also returned the portion of his beard he'd cut off and sent to them.

❋

Two mornings later, the Meehans kissed me goodbye and departed, well stocked with gin and toilet paper. They were heading back to Delhi for their flight to Britain. The day before, we'd been out walking and a Gujarati man asked if the Meehans were my wives.

"Kissin' cousins," said Marilyn.

"Sixty camels."

It took a moment for me to catch on. The man was about fifty and had the nose and eyes of a rooster. He wore a beige silk shirt buttoned at the collar and cuffs, and his belly threatened to burst his buttons. "Sixty camels for them?"

He tipped his head left-right-left, meaning yes.

I looked at the Meehans. "Hold out for seventy-five," said Marilyn.

❋

I pedalled a bike through Diu's high-walled streets on out through the city gate. The road was slender and sandy, and I passed through the speckled shade of tamarinds. To my right lay salt pans, to my left the village of Fudam and its church tower. Dogs howled as I rode up, and pigeons flapped as I entered the church. The birds resettled, but the stirred dust hung like centuries-old incense. Approaching the Madonna, I discovered she'd undergone a transformation: a *bhindi* on her forehead, her hair resculpted into a topknot, and her neck garlanded with marigolds. The Mother of Christ had gone Native.

Over the following days, I began to explore the island further. Apart from a few low hills in the middle, Diu was flat. The town of Goghla, at the opposite end of Diu, was a fishing village, its lanes filthy with guts and garbage. In between, there were grey beaches where dolphins came in close to shore, rolling like dark wheels through the flat sea. In the evenings, I returned regularly to one particular bar and talked to Luis, the owner. He was old and brusque and burly. He sat inside all day, lower lip drooping, looking crabby. When he opened a beer for a customer, he flung the cap clattering to the floor and swore in Portuguese. He missed the Portuguese, but at the same time he talked about what a bunch of bastards they were. He managed somehow to be simultaneously sullen and friendly. Luis remembered December 18, 1961, the day Nehru sent some two thousand soldiers to liberate Diu. Luis admitted that at first the people of Diu had welcomed the Indian army, but they soon changed their minds.

"Why?"

He blew a gust of air as if at a stupid question. "Because now everything is shit."

The responses to India's military action in Goa, Daman, and Diu were divided. Many quite naturally viewed it as liberation from the colonial yoke. Portugal was fascist, and civil liberties in Goa had been so restricted that nationalist agitators were jailed or deported to the African colonies. Loyalists and the foreign press, however, saw the reclamation of Goa as evidence of Nehru's hypocrisy. The press gleefully pointed its finger at the man who'd so often — and so self-righteously — pointed out the moral transgressions of others. The issue was not whether the colonies should be freed from Portugal but Nehru's use of violence in which thirty-eight men were killed. Furthermore, his political opponents saw this violence as having less to do with liberating Goa than with diverting attention from the fact that Nehru had done nothing when Chinese troops had occupied Indian territory in the northeast the previous year. Although the Chinese had withdrawn, the memory of the indignity remained, and it was Nehru who was judged at fault. He needed a victory to regain status, especially since an election was looming. Goa was it. So, he invaded. One cartoon showed a shark-like China swallowing India, which in turn gulped down the guppy-sized Goa.

There was another response to India's liberation of the Portuguese territories. Some claimed that after 450 years Goans had evolved a distinct culture and even ethnicity. They were no longer Indian. The answer was to hold a plebiscite. Portugal refused. (Just as India continues to refuse to hold one in Kashmir.) Given the two-thirds Hindu majority in Goa, the vote would undoubtedly have been for union with India. However, Goa's Hindus and Catholics were not evenly distributed. The majority of the 250,000 Catholics lived in what were called the Velhas Conquistas, the Old Conquests. They were composed of the districts of Ilhas, Salsete, and Bardez. In the first democratic assembly elections, in 1963, the population of the Old Conquests was "firmly against merger (with the neighbouring state of Maharashtra) and in favour of the concept of separate identity." The Old Conquests represented territory taken in the early 1500s, whereas the rest of Goa, the Novas Conquistas, the New Conquests, dated from 1763 to 1788. It appears that these 250 years were significant to the evolution of a sense of cultural distinctness.

One evening Luis asked me if I'd seen the tree in the quarry.

"No."

"Go look."

"Why?"

He was sitting drunk and sullen in the doorway of the shop, wearing a white cotton shirt and white cotton pants, a black rosary in his hand. He glared at me. He had no tolerance for insubordination. "Go. Listen."

So the next day I did. It was an old limestone quarry, near the cemetery, located out on that rocky plateau overlooking the ocean. The drop-off was so sudden that I didn't find the quarry until I nearly fell in. A twelve-metre tree stood in it. The tree's pale green leaves had silver undersides that shivered when the wind gusted. The tops of the branches were level with the surrounding ground, and I assumed the tree dated from 1961 when the Portuguese left and the quarry was abandoned. I searched until I found the crumbled steps, and soon I stood in a wide, dry excavation. My first impression was of how secure it felt, and how comfortable, what with the tan stone walls, the leafy bottom, and the tree stirring to life in the occasional wind. It was clean too. The locals didn't use it as a toilet. The stone for Diu's churches would have been cut from here. I saw the remains of a campfire. No doubt it was a popular place for kids to adventure, but there were no kids today, and it felt like an immensely solitary spot, as did all the land on this side of the island. In fact, all of Diu had the same sense of solitude about it, something rare in India, the second most populated country on the planet. Was this what Luis had wanted me to feel? Diu's *saudade*? Sitting in the quarry, I no longer heard the waves breaking on the cliffs. I was landlocked.

The Portuguese rarely ventured inland in their colonies. Like gauchos who felt lost away from the pampas, the Portuguese did not go far from the coast. This reluctance limited their empire and was no doubt a relief to the people who knew of them but did not have to meet them. Perhaps it had to do with the personality of a seagoing nation. An old irony sailors themselves admit is that they are in fact snailish, stay-at-home sorts, especially as they age. They carry their houses everywhere and so are always at home, even abroad. So with the Portuguese, who stayed near their ships, controlling sea lanes and ports but little else. By 1600 they had some fifty outposts. Eighty percent of their revenue from the East came not from trade but from the taxes they forced other cargo ships to pay for safe passage. And all ships had to buy *cartazes*, or "passes." The Portuguese were invincible at sea because their ships carried a variety of sails: square-rigged foresails, lateen-rigged mizzen, and many jibs — the combination of which allowed them to sail into the wind and gave them superior manoeuvrability.

Gusting wind stirred the tree, and I thought of it driving

the Portuguese ships. Many ships made direct voyages from Lisbon to India; half a year if all went well. Time enough for the hull to grow a flowing beard of algae, time enough for the passengers to get sick, recover, and get sick again, time enough for the stories to be told and retold until there was nothing more to say and nothing more to see but water and sky, water and sky. For variety there were the inevitable storms while rounding the cape and eventually the Indian coast.

The Portuguese were the last Crusaders, a spirit that was slow to die in Europe. In 1340, they took part in a victory over the Moors in Andalusia that ended North African intervention on the Peninsula. In 1365, Crusaders sacked Alexandria. In 1415, the combined Portuguese-Spanish forces of John I of Castile took Ceuta on the African mainland. Portugal's Prince Henry the Navigator and Alfonso d'Albuquerque both claimed their voyages were Crusades. Henry always got papal approval, and when he went to North Africa he carried a fragment of the "true" cross. The Muslims in the west were in retreat even as they advanced in the east. The Portuguese rode the turning tide. They sought pepper and souls and Prester John, the mythical Christian king whom they eventually decided lived in Coptic Ethiopia. They brought the Inquisition to Goa in 1550, carrying it like a virus, the way plague came with fleas on shipboard rats. The overseas clergy, led by Saint Francis Xavier, made mass conversions. What, I wonder, would Xavier think of the Somerset Maugham anecdote about the Goan Catholic priest who assured Maugham that of course they were faithful Christians, but first they were Hindus?

Between 1600 and 1773, the Inquisition in Goa examined

over 4,000 cases and burned 121 people, mostly native con-
verts and Jews, always the object of papal paranoia. Then
Portugal's Renaissance man, the Marquis de Pombal,
expelled the Inquisition from India. Pombal's intentions were
based as much upon economics as enlightenment. Good race
relations and the involvement of locals meant greater stability
and wealth. In fact, Pombal may have been the father of the
concept of affirmative action. A decree of 1761 stated that

> All my subjects born in Portuguese India and my other
> dominions in Asia, being baptized Christians . . . enjoy
> the same honours, dignities, prerogatives and privileges
> as those enjoyed by the natives of this kingdom
> [Portugal] without the slightest difference. Not only are
> they already qualified for all these honours, dignities,
> enterprises, posts, callings and jurisdictions, but I do
> seriously recommend to the viceroys of that state
> [India], its ministers and officials, that . . . preference be
> given to the natives of the respective territories, so long
> as they are qualified for them. . . .

I remained in the quarry until the ground was in shadow.
Higher up, where the sun still struck stone, the colour had
deepened to a golden ochre and the silhouette of the tree
spread like a map on the wall. Flocks of pigeons clapped past.
Sitting in that quarry, I felt Diu's entire Portuguese history,
423 years, closing in on me.

Later that evening, I told Luis I'd been to the quarry. He
treated me to a bottle of Kingfisher. Rosary looped around his

wrist, he went to a drawer behind the counter and found an old and deeply cracked photograph and handed it to me. It showed a man standing in front of an ornate antique carriage with gold-trimmed black wood and brass lanterns. I turned it over. I made out the words, written in Portuguese, Museo and Lisboa. It was the carriage museum in Lisbon. The date was 1974.

"My brother," said Luis.

※

I stayed on another week. Then another. Christmas passed. Christmas was celebrated to some degree all over India, acknowledged by both Muslims and Hindus. On Diu, the remaining Catholics emerged. I attended Midnight Mass on the 24th, for me an affair of confusion and nostalgia. For one strange moment I even considered taking communion. The ceremony's final gesture, wherein we turned and shook hands with those around us, moved me, for in that brief moment I was in contact with people from a distant land linked by an ancient faith. And, like it or not, I was born a Catholic, and its rituals were part of my childhood. I could deny them no more than I could the existence of my relatives. Some of those memories were both vivid and strange, as the time when I was eight years old and decided to do penance by putting pebbles in my shoes. I don't remember what sin I'd committed, maybe none at all. In fact, I suspect that I was just fantasizing over the saints and martyrs I'd heard about from the priest in the Saturday-morning catechism classes. Either way, something had apparently sunk in, so I gave it a go. It didn't last long. One step and I gave up on the glory of martyrdom. I also recall a picture book with selections from the Bible that included Daniel in the lions' den and some other guy in boiling oil. The guy in the oil was just standing there like he was in a hot tub — fully clothed — and chatting to the astounded Roman guards.

After Midnight Mass, we filed out into the hot Indian night. Dogs were howling. I passed a street-corner shrine set in a wall. Behind the small iron gates stood the Madonna and child amid candles. I found a long stick to fend off the dogs and, walking half the night, found six other such shrines, the candle flames, like a beleaguered faith, fighting the wind to stay alive.

TWO

In 1557, his fourth year in Goa, Camoens's fortunes took a brief turn for the better. During the fireworks celebration on behalf of the new viceroy, Dom Francisco Barreto, one of the rockets went awry and struck the galleon St. Matthew, *which had been drawn in close to shore and roofed with straw against the monsoon rain. In Camoens's own account,*

> the ship caught fire with such a blaze that it was terrifying — and it lay bulwark to bulwark with other ships drawn up alongside it. The wind was high and the flames leaped from one to another with such a tremendous roar and crackling that it seemed as though the whole city might be destroyed.

The new viceroy himself took charge of firefighting and was so heroic in his efforts that Camoens was inspired to write a play celebrating his courage.

The play was called Filodemo, *"loved by the people" in Greek, and of course earned Camoens immediate favour with Barreto. This was short-lived. An anonymous satire, critiquing the drunken behaviour of Portuguese officials at a celebration following the fire, was attributed to Camoens. He pleaded innocence and defended himself with a poem of his own, but no one was convinced. As a result, he was sent to Macao, near present-day Hong Kong, in the role of Trustee for the Dead and Absent — that is, executor of the wills and estates of dead or missing men. Yet his second exile turned out to be a bright spot for Camoens. Technically a punishment, in fact it provided him with an opportunity to make some money, something he hadn't been getting much of in India.*

He reached Macao on a merchant vessel built of Indian teak, one fitted with guns against pirates and loaded with wines, wool, dyes, crystal, clocks from Flanders, opium, shark skins, and sandalwood. It was an isolated existence for Camoens and the few Portuguese on Macao, as they were not allowed off the island to visit Canton, just 130 kilometres upriver. Still, his new position left him a lot of spare time, and he was now hard at work on The Lusiads. *And despite his red hair and beard, which must have made him an outlandish figure to the Chinese, he met a young and sympathetic Oriental woman. Her name, as best as he could pronounce it, was Dinamene, and here, for two years, he seemed to achieve contentment, until a certain Leonel de Sousa arrived.*

De Sousa felt cheated that he hadn't been given the post of Trustee for the Dead and Absent. He accused Camoens of embezzlement, which meant Camoens had to return to India and stand trial. On the voyage back the ship ran into a typhoon. They were off the coast of Cambodia at the time, at the mouth of the Mekong River. The wind ripped away one of the masts, leaving the ship wallowing. Life boats were swept away before they could be lowered. Camoens, clutching a sealed box containing his manuscripts, was swept overboard. His life's work clearly meant as much to him as his life itself, for he managed to hold onto the box and, clinging to a plank, made it to shore. What he did there, and how he survived, no one knows, but a year or so later — the time is uncertain — he reached Malacca and from there sailed back to Goa. The only written record Camoens left of his time shipwrecked on the Mekong is a stanza from The Lusiads:

> The Mekong will on its placid breast
> The drowning manuscript receive,
> Rescued from the misery of the wreck,
> And from the shoals, tempest-tossed, escaped.

Leonel de Sousa had also survived the shipwreck, and he was waiting. Guilty until proven innocent, Camoens went straight to prison. But de Sousa couldn't come up with any evidence, so Camoens was soon free to resume his marginal existence writing letters for the illiterate. Things had changed for the worse in Goa. The Inquisition had arrived, and Camoens no doubt witnessed the grotesque pageantry of the autos-da-fe, *which culminated with burning the victim at the stake. Another event that reflected the Portuguese attitudes of the time was the public destruction of a Buddhist relic captured in Ceylon. The relic was reputed to be one of the Buddha's teeth. The viceroy, Dom Constantine de Braganza, in his wisdom, sent it to the archbishop, who ground it up in a mortar, burned the powder, and then proceeded through the crowd to the river, where he dumped the ashes.*

Of more personal consequence for Camoens, however, was the news that Catherine de Ataide was dead. His response was the most famous sonnet in the Portuguese language:

Gentle spirit mine,
Thou who didst depart this earth
Before thy time,
May'st thou be given rest eternal
With the bless'd,
Though I still abide in anguish
On this earth.
If, where thou dwellest
In the realm on high,
Memory be granted of this, our mortal life,
Forget not, I beg,
This heart that yearns within its breast for thee,
Nor the pure passion that flames so ardent
In these eyes.
If thou findest aught of worth
In this great love of mine that knows no cure,
Pray God, who cut thy mortal years so short,
At once to bear me hence to where thou art,
And, swift as thy sweet form was snatched from me,
May I once more behold thy features dear,
And feast upon them with these hungry eyes.

It's a poem that does more than just survive the test of time. It crystallizes Camoens's loss and isolation so far from home, feelings every traveller endures.

Cow eating cardboard (Calcutta)

BOMBAY 1990

I left Diu by bus, intending to get off at Daman. Of Goa, Diu, and Daman, the most innocuous was Daman. Situated just off the truck-clogged road that ran from Surat to Bombay, it lacked Goa's reputation and Diu's setting. When we arrived, it was four in the morning, and I'd been on the bus for twenty hours. Four hours more and we'd be in Bombay. I was tempted to skip Daman, but, just as the bus was pulling out, I got off.

Daman's historical importance lay in its position, almost directly east of Diu, at the opposite side of the Gulf of Cambay. The Portuguese took Daman in 1531 so that ships patrolling between Diu and Daman could control access to the gulf and all its trade. Like that of Diu, Daman's main source of income nowadays was from liquor sales.

At four in the morning, the mosquitoes were out in full force, turning my hunt for a hotel into misery. I walked the streets of Daman for three hours, waking night porters who gazed at me through iron grilles and shook sleepy heads, until the sun began to rise through a burlap-coloured haze. Every hotel was full. Even the taxi drivers, notorious liars who'd drive you around for hours insisting they knew of a room, said all the rooms were full.

One driver, whose gold teeth gleamed in the dome light of his Ambassador, said "Muslims." And he made a drinking motion. He meant that the place was packed with Muslims come to drink. The driver's name was Ved. He explained that

Daman was divided into two halves, Nani Daman ("Little Daman") and Moti Daman ("Big Daman"). He drove me to the fort and then across a bridge spanning a sewer masquerading as a river, through the town wall, to the steps of the cathedral, which was shut up. I got out and strolled around. There were the smells of wood smoke and damp stone, sea water and sewer. Birds shrilled in a tree, and kids in blue-and-white uniforms ran shouting to school, while a man bicycled past with two oars over his shoulder. Eventually, Ved dropped me at the train station ten kilometres away, at Vapi.

❁

By the time I reached Bombay, that brief morning idyll had been smothered in the pollution and poverty of the metropolis. I got a room near Bombay's Victoria Terminus railway station. The architecture of VT station is categorized as Victorian Gothic. I found the place Gothic inside as well. People were lying on the floors in every imaginable attitude, their crates and bundles stacked around them. Some looked terminally ill, others joked and cooked. Long lines led to the ticket windows. In the offices, supervisors, subsupervisors, and assistant supervisors sat about sipping tea. As for the toilet attendant in VT station, here was the man with the world's worst job. I don't know how long he'd been there, but he needed a vacation. He sat on a stool inside the washroom, his face pinched in a permanent grimace against the stink. His expression said "My world is a toilet. Everywhere I look I see people pissing. And over there, behind that wall, they do the other thing. I smell them, and I hear them. I watch them come in, and I watch them go out." His was a job to corrode the soul. Toilet attendant. Yet toilet was too delicate a word for such a dismal reality. Urinal? No. *Pissoir?* Better. Bog? Close. Shitter? Almost. He existed in a world of bladders and bowels, piss, shit, and flatulence. Seated on his stool, he watched men fish out their hoses, set their feet, fart, sigh, and gush against the wall. Maybe he didn't smell it anymore. Maybe he'd become immune. His expression said otherwise. He smelled it. It was there in his nostrils all day. He breathed it in and he breathed it out. The smell pervaded his clothes, his hair, the very pores of his skin. Perhaps he'd become philosophical: We are but intestines on legs, digestive tracts with feet. A waiter watches over the eating, which is one end of the process; I watch over the defecating, which is the other end of the process. The waiter and I, therefore, are as the right hand and the left. . . . This might earn him a chuckle from his friends, especially given the Indian tradition of eating with the right, while the left is reserved for another purpose.

And what did the Indians make of this fellow? An example of jolly bad karma? Tough luck? Bad break? You must have been a right bastard in your previous life, eh? Yet from what I could see, most people just rushed in to relieve themselves and then rushed right back out without seeing him at all. He was merely part of the facility, like the faucets and the floors. In his place, I'd take to robbing tourists like me.

Work was not easy to get in India, and even when you got it the pay was bad. On the bus from Jaipur to Jaisalmer, for example, we'd passed roadwork where infants played alongside their parents, who dug ditches and raked gravel. The adults earned approximately fifty cents US a day. Field labourers earned between thirty and seventy cents per day. And *bidi* rollers made a daily wage ranging from forty to seventy cents for rolling 800 cigarettes.

Devising bad jobs is one way India tries to deal with its massive unemployment. I recall a Calcutta bookshop that had one man to open the door, a second to take my pack and give me a number, a third to give me a chit when I found what I wanted, a fourth to take the chit when I paid and then supply me with yet another chit, and a fifth to take that chit and hand me my purchase. On the way out, I returned the number to the man who'd attended my pack, and then, finally, the fellow at the door fulfilled his function and opened it as I went out. It was the same with upscale restaurants, which had doormen, cloakroom attendants, water waiters, cutlery waiters, plate waiters, napkin waiters, headwaiters, assistant headwaiters, waiters-in-training, and others whose functions were too subtle for me to understand. Lord Mountbatten, the last viceroy of India, had a staff of 7,500, including a permanently employed chicken plucker. (In the hot season, when he went up into the mountains to the viceregal lodge in Simla, he brought along a skeleton staff of 350.) Yet it was not simply a matter of inventing jobs and then handing them out. Nothing is straightforward in India. Leonard Mosley, in his book *The Last Days of the British Raj*, relates an anecdote indicating the intricate relationship between job function and caste. Apparently, just before a banquet, Lady Linlithgow's dog did its business on the carpet. She called for a servant to clean it up, yet it took so long to find one of low enough rank to do it

Irony

that she was on her knees herself scrubbing away when the guests began to arrive.

❈

Outside VT station, the sidewalks were jammed with stalls and carts, and you could buy anything from underpants to Donald Duck wristwatches. I walked to the India Gate, an imposing arch built to commemorate the visit of George V in 1935. It struck me, fifty-five years later, as a symbol of colonial oppression, something the Indians might want to tear down, but then again it served as a nice shady place to pee. It stands at the waterfront, where a tout with eyes the colour of bile offered to show me "clean Bombay and dirty Bombay."

"Dirty Bombay?"

He stepped closer and lowered his voice. "Women in cages," he said, referring to the red-light district.

"And where is clean Bombay?"

He looked at me like I was an idiot. "Clean Bombay is here."

I declined his help and entered the Taj Mahal Hotel, where both Indians and foreigners go to pretend they're not in India at all. Inside was an air-conditioned mall with travel agents, shops, a pharmacy where you could renew your Valium prescription, and a bookstore.

Later that afternoon, I wandered along the waterfront looking at the fishing boats, the ferries, and the freighters anchored in the oily water. Four and a half centuries ago, when the Portuguese sailed in, they declared the bay good, and Mumbai became Bombay. They held it until 1661, when they handed it over to the British as part of Catherine of Braganza's dowry when she married Charles II of England. Yet nearly two centuries of British control did not, in the opinion of adventurer and linguist Sir Richard Francis Burton, improve Bombay, which he described as "a low, black, dirty port."

That first night in my hotel room — an outrageous thirteen dollars — I was lying on the bed when a movement on the ceiling caught my eye. The ceiling was white and decorated in a waffle iron pattern, with raised squares alternating with inset squares. I'd already noticed that one of these squares was missing. Now a rat was peering down at me through the hole. I picked up my shoe and swung at it. The rat bared its teeth — horribly long yellow teeth. I backed away, looked around, grabbed one of my socks, and plugged the hole. The odd thing to me was not all these rats in themselves but that I didn't remember seeing any on previous trips. I suspect that the spectacle of Calcutta, where I'd first entered India in 1979 at the age of twenty-three, overshadowed these lesser sights. Lying on that bed in Bombay beneath the sock-bunged ceiling, with my shoe in my hand ready to defend myself, I thought back to those first few impressions of Calcutta, a city sunk so spectacularly in decrepitude.

I remembered, for instance, the sadhu, the holy man, I saw in the chai shop on Chowringhee Road, Calcutta's Oxford Street. I knew the mud caking his shoulder-length hair prevented lice. I knew his eyes were yellow because of too much *ganja*. And I guessed the bottle of Limca simply meant he was thirsty. All this made sense. But why the studded black leather biker's jacket? It was thirty degrees Celsius. More to the point,

Calcutta market

why was a holy man wearing leather, an animal skin, maybe even the skin of a cow, the animal sacred to Hindu India?

I got bold. I greeted the sadhu.

"Namaste, baba."

He reacted like a marionette tugged to attention. He faced me, eyes glowing as hot as kilns. He put his palms together. "Namaste!" Then he sang in Hindi, gripping the table as if otherwise he'd fly up. The fierce voice soared from his pelvis right up through his throat: Man calling to God, or rather God calling through Man. It lasted perhaps one minute. Then he sank into silence. The proprietor continued reading the newspaper behind the counter. The fans continued twirling. No one else was in the narrow, high-ceilinged café. When I left, the sadhu nodded once, imperiously, as though I were dismissed.

At the time, I was staying at the Astoria on Sudder Street, an involuntary splurge at four dollars a night, all the cheaper places being full. The Astoria didn't possess the grandeur of faded glory, but it had character, and it had Prakash: bellhop, waiter, handyman, procurer. Prakash looked like he was seventy but, as is so often the case in India, was much younger. His habit of walking straight-spined and tall enhanced his dignity, even though the gold piping of his waiter's jacket had been reduced to threads. He went everywhere barefoot. Whenever he stepped off the Astoria premises, he wrapped a brown blanket about his shoulders. Stick-skinny, his bones and sockets clicked and shifted like levers and pulleys under his skin. I was fascinated by him, especially when he performed those Indian hand gestures that look simultaneously so elegant and dismissive, as though he possessed absolute certainty about the positions of the Earth and the sky and everything in between.

Each morning, in the dining room, Prakash served the breakfast of cardboard cornflakes, pasty toast, and tooth-staining tea. The pot and cups were chipped and yellowed and to me suggested antique dentures. When he was done, Prakash would return to the kitchen and squat before his own breakfast, a pile of rice and vegetables on a sheet of newspaper that he ate with the chopstick fingers of his right hand.

Sudder Street hypnotized me. Whole families camped on the sidewalks. Barbers squatted on the side of the road and scraped throats with rusty straight razors, picked wax from ears with pins, tweezed nose and ear hairs. All day a legless beggar sang on a corner, next to the women who lined up to fill plastic pails at a pump. And there were the rickshaw wallahs who pulled their antiquated contraptions. Calcutta is one of the last cities to employ a full fleet of hand-pulled rickshaws. It was sobering to see a twig-limbed man straining barefoot through the sewerish streets pulling not one but two fat and belching businessmen back to the office after their lunch of goat curry. It presented a dilemma: if you decided to be indignantly humanitarian and refused to use rickshaws, then the men didn't make money and their families didn't eat.

My second day in Calcutta, I saw someone who would remain forever in my memory as the Man on the Sidewalk. He wasn't on Sudder Street but across town in a more affluent area. He wasn't a beggar, not any longer at least. Whoever he was, and whatever he had been, the Man on the Sidewalk was dying, that was clear, and I couldn't help but look, even though pedestrians flowed past him as if he was nothing but a stone in a stream. He was about twenty, with grey skin shrunk so taut to his jaw I could describe the contours of his teeth. He stared up at the boardwalk's wooden ceiling as if awed by a vision of fiery angels.

He was no longer in this world, and that's what fascinated me. I walked back and forth past him to get a good look. Then, feeling guilty, I left. But I went back the next afternoon, and he was still there. I didn't do anything because no one else seemed to be doing anything. Naïve, new to India, I assumed steps had already been taken and aid was on the way. I also noticed that no one tossed coins to him, which said a lot. Why waste them? the locals seemed to be saying. Calcuttans presumably develop a discerning eye in these matters.

The number of Calcutta's destitute is debated, as is the city's population, but of the approximately eight million people in 1979 one million homeless was considered a conservative estimate. Most lived in Howrah, Calcutta's "other side of the tracks." But the Man on the Sidewalk was in a business district that had few beggars. He lay at an angle across the boardwalk, arms stiff as fallen branches, his fingertips missing. I hadn't noticed that detail the day before. And, like the day before, I went away in tears, but I was ecstatic too, secretly thrilled by what I was seeing. He was dying, and I was getting to watch.

I felt guilty of course and told myself I wasn't going back. And again the idea of actually doing something to help him impressed itself upon me. But where to begin in a place as chaotic as Calcutta? So I told Prakash about him, yet Prakash

Calcutta

simply tipped his head left-right-left in that peculiarly Indian gesture and said "Yes." The Man on the Sidewalk was hardly news to him. He was to me, though. The only dead person I'd ever seen at that point was my grandfather, lying in a coffin clasping a crucifix in both hands, a look of concentration on his face as if willing himself to the next world. The Man on the Sidewalk wasn't quite dead, he was teetering, and he was abandoned; these facts made him fascinating. I couldn't stop thinking about him. I lay in my hotel room and imagined visiting him before dawn, when the street was empty and I could have him to myself. I'd talk to him in a low voice, confident he could hear me, confident he was someone I could ask about the future, about how to live, because he was facing the ultimate event, because he had absolute perspective — one foot in this world and one in the next.

I went back the third day, and he'd shrunk, lips gone, eyes dry, and his fingertips shorter still. And then I understood — rats.

"Oh, so many rats, sahib, so many rats," chanted Prakash as he lay poison along the Astoria's halls.

Did I finally act? Yes, I found a police station and reported the man's condition. When I entered the station, big dark-eyed guys gripping *lathi* sticks — metre-long clubs — confronted me. When I explained why I was there, they nodded and said they knew, it was being taken care of.

And apparently it was, for on the fourth day he was gone. I felt relieved and at the same time disappointed, because I'd got a taste of something and wanted more. I also knew that in Calcutta there existed the exact place to find more: Mother

Teresa's hospital. I decided to visit it, telling myself the convenient half-lie that I was sympathetic, that I wanted to help. So off I went, my mind scampering on ahead, almost giddy with anticipation. I imagined Mother Teresa's Hospital for the Dying as a place of calm, an antechamber of Paradise, where people of profound dignity were relieved at this final release from a life that had been, after all, hell. I wanted to experience death from the safe place of life. I wanted to watch. I wanted to get high on their deaths.

Halfway there I turned around. Not only from guilt and embarrassment, but also because I had nothing to offer. To gawk was invasive and vulgar, it would make me feel lousy about myself, and it certainly wouldn't do much to improve the lot of the people there.

On the way back, I wandered slowly along the river, feeling drained by a late-afternoon lassitude made all the worse by the heat. Barges and freighters rode their anchors, and enormous iron buoys marked the channel. A launch dangerously overburdened with passengers set out with only inches of freeboard. The Howrah Bridge arched across on its blackened girders. Eighty kilometres south, the river branched through the Sunderbans, a marshy jungle where each year the Bengal tiger ate a few villagers. It was low tide. Women bathed in the brown water, their gold saris streaming out on the current. Their children, meanwhile, lay on the bank fanning their arms up and down making dark angels in the mud.

❋

Twelve years later, in a thirteen-dollar room in Bombay, I

woke with my shoe next to me on the bed. I checked my toes and fingers. They were intact. The rat had been forced to find other sources of protein. I left my sock wedged in the hole and went out to get some breakfast.

The Leopold II seemed a strange name for a Bombay restaurant. It was high-ceilinged and noisy with both Indians and foreigners, and the waiters used their aluminum serving trays to beat back the beggars and touts. I found a table by the wall and watched the show. A Japanese couple in their twenties entered. Both wore their hair in dreadlocks, and both wore psychedelic baggies, embroidered Rajastani vests, rings, bangles, anklets, necklaces, earrings, and ornate shoulder bags. They were identical in everything except that he walked with a staff and had a beard composed of about ten long black hairs. His staff was a two-metre length of gnarled wood with an amulet on top. They sat down and lit *bidis*, smoking them Indian style, through their fists. Dangling from their necks were pendants containing photos of Bhagwan Shri Rajneesh, who, it so happened, had died just a week before, on January 19, 1990, in Poona. I'd followed the Bhagwan's antics in his ashram in Antelope, Oregon, and had often thought of driving down the coast from Vancouver to have a look at the setup. Now I had my chance. It would be easy to stop in Poona en route to Goa, so after a couple of days in Bombay I headed southeast.

The train service was excellent. I got a recliner in an airconditioned car and four hours later was in the National Hotel, directly across the road from the Poona station, where painters were at work on some of the rooms. The manager was a vast and dignified gent. The hotel supplied not one but two

towels, plus a bar of soap. At five dollars a night, I expected
nothing less. Not having to use my own towel always made me
feel ahead of the game. Unlike socks or a T-shirt, towels, like
blue jeans, are awkward to wash in hotel sinks, and they take a
long time to dry. For years I'd been working to reduce the contents of my bag to the bare essentials: one pair of pants, one pair
of shorts that doubled as a bathing suit, and maybe two shirts.
As for underwear, they were an ongoing dilemma. Just how nec-
essary were they? I was particularly proud of having made the
leap from backpack to daypack. My goal was to reduce it all to
a shoulder bag. To me this equalled freedom. No more shoulders aching from lack of circulation, no more need to submit my
pack to thieving baggage handlers at airports, no more need to
chain my pack to a post on the trains while I slept. The next step
was to go naked. A *sanyasan* walking the Earth.

After completing my rat check, I showered, then headed off
on foot to the Rajneesh Ashram. Poona was flat and polluted
and nothing much to look at. It was a business town, and from
what I'd read Rajneesh was a businessman. The first thing I
saw when I reached the ashram gates was a Sikh taxi driver
and a Westerner in red robes swinging at each other. The Sikh
was fat and the Westerner scrawny, and they pawed at each
other more than punched.

I said to a young woman, "What happened?"

"Money, man, whataya think?" Then she smelled something — me, apparently. She sniffed me and sneered, "You eat
meat." She stepped away for a better view of the fight.

The Sikh got in a good left and the Westerner dropped to his
butt. Then the Sikh moved in and kicked, yet lost his balance

and went down hard on his hip. The Westerner got up and landed a kick of his own, but his Birkenstocks weren't exactly biker boots. He hopped on his good leg and howled over his hurt toes. The Sikh lay groaning. The crowd of red-robed Westerners seemed let down that the action had ended so soon.

I asked a middle-aged American couple if the ashram could survive now that Rajneesh was gone. The man tipped his head back and laughed loudly, a little too loudly I thought, as if the laugh string on his back had been pulled. The woman said that Rajneesh was in them all now; the community was charged and strengthened by having absorbed his spirit. Rajneesh had been renamed Osho, meaning "great teacher" in Japanese. The woman recited his epitaph: "Osho/Never Born/Never Died/Only Visited This Planet Earth Between Dec. 11, 1931 – Jan. 19, 1990."

To be honest, I sympathized when Rajneesh got the bum's rush out of Antelope, Oregon. What had he done but beat the Americans at their own game and become ridiculously rich? I recalled a statement once made by talk show host Johnny Carson. Asked whether he seriously thought he was worth the million dollars a year he made, he said "This is America. If I make it, I'm worth it." Unless, it seemed, you were a little brown man with a funny accent who convinced well-educated Americans to unburden themselves of their wealth by passing it over to him.

Surrounded by walls and hedges four and a half metres high, the ashram was located in Koregon Park, an elite Poona neighbourhood resplendent with Victorian mansions and Mediterranean villas. And Koregon Park was surrounded by the usual squalor of every Indian city, which made the ashram even more Edenic, a Shangri-La in a slum. It drew many people with many motives: the sincere seekers, the horny hunting that fabled free sex, the Latins who managed to look chic in their robes, the sad women and the lonely men whose uncertainty was betrayed by their trembling eyes. And there were the inevitable Kashmiri merchants who lined the approach, selling shawls and silver and swearing upon their honour that you had to buy today, for tomorrow — alas! — they returned to their fabled vale. An old woman with four bald dogs begged as near to the marble entrance as she was permitted. Six barefoot men pushed a wooden-wheeled cart loaded with steel construction rods. And the Rajneesh devotees themselves — pale shins protruding beneath their robes, pale toes snug as fatted grubs in their Birkenstocks — discussed what all sojourners to the mystic East discussed: the exchange rate and the state of their stool.

To stay in the ashram, you had to show the gatekeepers proof of a negative result on an AIDS test. I opted for the tour. My guide was a Swiss woman of about sixty. I asked why she was in the ashram.

"Because I feel happy here."

She walked slowly, savouring every step and every breath. I liked her. Immediately inside, we followed a stone path through a Japanese garden. We passed people meditating, reading, chatting, a guy on his back on a bench snoring, and a lone woman weeping. Another guy leaned over a rock pool, languidly caressing the water as if having never before experienced such a miracle of nature. In the marble-floored meditation hall, musicians plucked sitars, preparing for their evening performance. People walked arm-in-arm; people met and embraced. Their robes flowed, the music drifted like incense, all was harmony, all pristine, and everyone's eyes were as glazed as doughnuts. My teeth began to ache with the sweetness of it all. I began to see the ashram as the village in *The Prisoner* and expected Patrick McGoohan to ride up in a golf cart while evil laughter echoed over hidden speakers.

My guide took my arm. "Relax. We're not all zombies."

We entered the bookshop, which was filled with Rajneesh tapes, books, videos, transcripts, posters, and calendars. There was also a post office and a Japanese restaurant. The list went on: gymnasium, therapy rooms, courses, workshops; there were even plans for an Olympic-sized swimming pool, and best of all everyone was AIDS-free.

The Rajneesh Ashram reminded me of Copan *gompa*, in Kathmandu, a Tibetan Buddhist monastery in which I'd spent two months in the winter of 1979. I was twenty-three at the time, and in those days enthusiastically Buddhist. I had no doubt that Buddhism was the best religion. It was clean and serene and without contradictions. Yet in the monastery I learned a few sobering things, and not just about my beloved Buddhism. I learned, for instance, that neither the "world" nor the ego is necessarily left behind upon entering a spiritual retreat. Cliques and elitism adapted like viruses and flourished in those rarefied atmospheres. For example, it was a mistake to mention transcendental meditation, for it was sneered at as the McDonald's of spirituality. And if you were misguided enough to be a Christian, you would be informed that you were, in fact, a Buddhist — you just hadn't evolved enough to realize it.

In Copan I'd taught some English. One of my students tended to fall asleep. I tried not taking this personally, but I did mention this habit to another teacher. She was horrified.

"Never let them fall asleep in the afternoon. They'll build up the karma of creatures with the same slothful habits!"

I tried getting this straight. "You mean he'll get, like, dog karma?"

"Dog karma, exactly!"

The Copan monastery sat atop a hill. As I recall, its setting was about all that was conventional. When I first walked out to have a look, I saw a guy at the foot of the hill wearing nothing but limp undershorts, boxing with a Nepali woman. She clenched her veil between her teeth and held one hand behind her back, like she'd bet she could whip him that way. She was doing a good job. They circled each other by a stream. When I got closer, I saw she held a bar of soap behind her — his bar of soap. He was skinny, bald, and bearded. She had a bull ring through her nose, a stud in one nostril, and seven or eight hoops in her ear. She wasn't giving up that soap. Women holding tubs of laundry on their hips cheered her on. I continued up the hill, and near the top got attacked by a two-legged dog. It ran at me with ugly agility, butt bouncing and skidding over the dirt, yet a flung stone sent the dog into a spin before it got its teeth into me. A bald boy in robes grabbed the dog by the tail and wheelbarrowed it off down the path. The dog, I'd later learn, was a sort of mascot.

Meanwhile, I looked around. So, this was a Buddhist

monastery. A couple of mud-brick buildings with corrugated roofs, clapboard dorms, and, rising above all, a round tower. Mountains encircled the valley, and the Himalayas stood snow-peaked and spectacular in the blue-black distance.

I went up smooth steps, opened the tower door, and discovered two men deep in conversation. They sat cross-legged, one an old hippie, the other a monk, a lama, with a big head and saffron robes. As I opened the door, the lama looked up and smiled, showing widely-spaced buck teeth, and waved me in like I was an old friend. He offered me a cushion, and I sat down. They continued talking in Nepalese or Tibetan, I had no idea which. Every few minutes the lama gave me a big grin as if it was splendid, just splendid, that I'd come. And damn if he didn't seem to mean it. So I sat there on my flat red cushion. I relaxed. I felt good. Actually, I started feeling more than good, I felt relieved. I was twenty-three and exhausted. I'd just come from two months of rather unBuddhistic indulgence in Thailand, and felt not only burnt out and guilty, but confused. Lama Thupten Yeshe was forty-four and vibrant. He also had a heart condition. Yet that didn't show, and his ease was utterly natural. The key seemed not what he had but what he didn't have: contrivance. He was here, as simply and openly as that. The reassuring strength of his presence was refreshing, and I immediately felt that pretence with him would have been blasphemous. So I sat there, not sure at the time who he was but certain I wanted to know. That was Day One.

Day Two I was left under the sincere, though melancholy, guidance of Adrian Feldman, a medical doctor from Melbourne. He'd given up medicine for religion because he felt that Buddhism was a more effective way to alleviate suffering. Adrian never looked relaxed in robes. He looked like a woman perpetually worried that her skirt was too short. He was stooped under the weighty obligation of achieving enlightenment in this life. As he told a group of us in the meditation hall, "You may not get another human incarnation for countless *kalkas*, so don't waste your time talking about Carlos Castaneda." A *kalka* was ten thousand years.

There were twenty of us. I kept glancing around for Yeshe, assuming Adrian was just the warm-up act. The meditation hall was floored with old carpets, and Adrian sat cross-legged on the dais, his skull shaved bathing-cap white. Behind him hung a *tankha*, a cloth painting depicting Chenrezig, god of compassion. Adrian slowly poured the strung beads of his *mala*, his Buddhist rosary, from one hand to the other.

"The world is maya. Illusion. The 'I' is an illusion, a useful illusion, but it has no self-existent being."

Heinrich, the guy I'd seen boxing with the Nepali woman, disagreed. "The 'I' is as solid as any pain."

"Exactly," said Adrian. "Buddhism is liberation from the pain of the 'I.'"

Heinrich threw his arms wide. "Pain is all we have! Pain and passion!"

"Be passionate about meditation, but don't fall in love with it."

Heinrich was aghast. "What's wrong with love?"

"Love is wonderful. But don't fall in love with love."

"I thought Buddhism was the happy religion. You sound like a Catholic!"

Adrian let that pass. He spoke of rebirth and the thousands of lives we waste wandering the lesser incarnations, which included being born female.

June, an East Indian woman from Vancouver, whose braces were the envy of the nose-ringed local women, interrupted. "Why is being born female a lesser incarnation than being born male?"

"Because as a woman you have less freedom, and therefore less opportunity to meet the dharma, and the dharma is the way to enlightenment."

Yet here she was, in a Buddhist monastery, meeting the dharma, and she said so. "I'm here, aren't I?"

Adrian acknowledged this detail but patiently insisted she was missing an essential point. "You're a Westerner."

"Then Buddhism has nothing to say to women or non-Asians at all."

"It has a great deal to say."

June read aloud from the *Lam Rim*, a ninety-page booklet we'd been issued, on the basic tenets of Mahayana Buddhism. *"If you covet your neighbour's wife, you'll be reborn as an iron-beaked bird."* She looked up. "Are you joking?"

"You have to appreciate that was originally aimed toward Tibetan peasants."

June made a show of looking around. "I don't see any Tibetan peasants."

Adrian saw he was losing her. "Why are you here then? Something brought you."

June couldn't deny that.

Luc, a strange case who claimed to have walked all the way

from Marseille to Kathmandu, suddenly woke from his nap. He stretched his legs before him like a child, looked around, and said, "I come from France by feet."

Adrian indulged him. "That's excellent, Luc, excellent."

❋

Later, I talked to June. We strolled between the flooded rice paddies that sat like mirrors in the earth reflecting the afternoon sky.

She said, "I didn't want to say I'm here because it's the cheapest place in Kathmandu."

I confessed that I too considered that a major point in Copan's favour. "But that's not the only reason."

"Oh, no!"

"Well?"

Despite debating Adrian to the wall, she couldn't say exactly why she was here.

I told her about Yeshe, and she got excited. "Yes! I want to meet someone like him."

Yet Yeshe didn't appear that day either. It was just us, Heinrich, June, Luc, and the others, which included sixty kids living at Copan, all bald, all robed, all filthy, all smiling. I got to know one of them, Danzan. His dilemma was obvious — he was sixteen. Furthermore, the foreigners passing through made him realize he lived in a backwater, albeit an exotic one. They passed in a procession of Rolling Stones T-shirts, Levis, and Nikes, all talking of Goa, Phuket, Kuta Beach, the number of credits they needed to complete their psychology degrees, and of someone named Annie Hall. They talked of movies as if

such things were as common as shoes. Danzan had never seen
a movie, and he didn't own a pair of shoes, but his English was
good. He might someday travel overseas as an interpreter. This
hope made life bearable. Meanwhile, he was sixteen, stuck in
that limbo between kid and adult, East and West.

I asked him about Lama Yeshe. "Where is he?"

"Gone."

"Gone? Where?"

"Dharamsala."

I was crushed. "When's he coming back?"

Danzan shrugged. He had other things on his mind.
"What's a frog?"

"A frog? A small green animal. A reptile. It jumps."

This troubled Danzan. He wrinkled his forehead. He had
a round, rugged, Oriental face. He pointed to Heinrich and
said, "He called that man over there a frog." Danzan pointed
to Luc. "Is it because he jumps?"

The next afternoon I met Adrian coming down the steps
from the tower where I'd met Yeshe. I told him of the meeting.

"That's a good sign. An omen. He called you. He's a great
lama. Immensely compassionate." Adrian held up the aluminum plate he was carrying. "I've been feeding his rat."

I thought I'd heard wrong. "His cat?"

Adrian smiled fondly. "His rat. It lives under his bed. He
won't let any harm come to it." Then Adrian frowned. "I'm
afraid Yeshe will get bitten, so I've been trying to convince him
to let it go in the fields, but he says no." Adrian looked at me.
"He should be dead."

"The rat?"

"No, no. Yeshe. Doctors examined him last year. The valves in his heart. When they told him, he just smiled and thanked them." Adrian looked past me. I followed his gaze. Copan had a view of the rice paddies all around. Some were dry, some were flooded, and others were hazed a pale green with young rice shoots. Adrian said, "Nepal is beautiful in the spring."

"Yes, it is."

"He's not a reincarnate lama, you know. He's done it all in this life." Adrian blew a long sigh and shook his head in admiration. We watched that two-legged dog drag itself across the dirt toward the cookhouse. "It used to attack cattle. So a farmer slashed its legs. Yeshe took it in."

I thought about that, a lame dog and a pet rat.

Yeshe didn't return during my time at Copan. And over the next month the group degenerated into backbiting and one-upmanship. We'd sneak off to Kathmandu to gorge on pie and smoke hash and then return, as chagrined and ridiculous as only lost Westerners with too much time and money can be. Heinrich started sleeping with June, and I was jealous. When it was all over, I flew to Sri Lanka. On the east coast, in Trincomalee, I found some solace in the money I was saving — room and board, and even a beer or two each night, never totalled more than two and a half dollars.

❉

Now, in Poona, I was no longer a Buddhist, and certainly not a Rajneeshi, though Lama Yeshe remained vivid in my memory. When I left the Rajneesh Ashram, I wandered back across

Poona to my hotel. I found the door to my room wide open, and two men inside painting the walls with sawed-off brooms.

Unable to think of anything better to say, I asked them what they were doing.

"Painting," said one, smiling glassily. Fumes seemed to be doing to these boys what the Bhagwan had done to a lot of Westerners.

"Why?"

"Manager."

There was a tarp over the bed, and my pack had been chucked in a corner and was now speckled with pale green paint. I backed out, already lightheaded. The manager was sipping tea in the lobby. I complained. He called for tea. When it came, I held the cup and saucer in my hand and spoke of the chemicals in paint, the toxicity, the danger to the lungs and the brain. He listened politely. I concluded my rant by demanding another room.

"All the other rooms are occupied."

"All of them?"

"All."

"How about the roof?"

"The roof is not safe."

When I'd arrived, I'd noticed that the train station was also the bus station for points south, including Goa. I got my pack, wiped off the spatters of paint, and headed across the road. At ten that night I was on a bus south to Margao, Goa's second city after Panjim, the capital.

By morning we were descending the Western Ghats to the tropical coast. The transition was abrupt. We left the high, dry

Deccan Plateau and entered lush green grass, coconut palms, waxy-leafed banana trees, and wet air weighted with the scents of shrubs and flowers. Soon we were passing small white-washed churches.

Measuring about one hundred kilometres north to south, with an area of roughly 1,400 square kilometres, Goa was smaller than the island of Oahu, and its population was about a million and a half. As for Margao, it looked as dilapidated and nondescript as any Indian town, the remnants of its Portuguese architecture collapsing as quickly as heat and neglect could do the job.

I got a bus to Colva beach, about ten kilometres away, plodded down to the sea with my pack, and stood there. The water glittered like crushed glass. The shore was lined with cafés built of bamboo and palm leaves. It was 9 a.m., and reggae pounded from every one of them. Touts were already busy flogging jewelry and sarongs to the sunbathers. A middle-aged man in a loincloth approached me. He was carrying a wire rack that held jingling bottles of tinted oils.

"Massage, sahib?"

"No thanks."

He pulled what looked like a knitting needle from a shoulder bag. "Ear cleaning?"

"No."

"Hearing will improve hundred percent. Guaranteed."

I could see other touts struggling through the soft sand toward me. I retreated up the road, and all morning I wandered Colva's back streets — quiet and shady beneath enormous banyan trees — and eventually found a room in the guesthouse of Clementina Mesquita and her brother Jorge. They were devout Catholics. Three photographs of Pope John Paul II hung on the living room wall, an iron crucifix a metre and a half high leaned like an anchor in a corner, and in the opposite corner stood an altar whose log-sized candles illuminated a nativity. My own room had a six-metre-high ceiling and a red tile floor. The curtain rod was held by two carved, death-white hands protruding straight from the wall. The gruesomeness rather appealed to me.

Both Clementina and Jorge drifted about in a Catholic melancholy I recognized from my own Sunday mornings in church. Over the next few weeks, I discovered that the heat and humidity added to the mood of lassitude. All this, in turn, seemed to deepen the pervading nostalgia so many Goans felt for the Portuguese.

Again and again people spoke of the good old days. And in Clementina Mesquita's case the nostalgia had a personal element. In 1961, she and a Portuguese man were in love. They wanted to marry. Yet his family wouldn't allow it because she was of mixed blood. When Nehru drove the Portuguese out of Goa that year, Clementina said she'd never go with another. And she never did. At forty-five, she was potbellied and handsome, wore a black frock and a rosary around her wrist, and had the mournful eyes of an icon.

Her brother had a reputation for going on a bender every month or so on cashew fenny, wherein he drank himself out of the despair he otherwise locked inside. When I met Jorge, he was holding a bloody machete under his arm and half a snake in each fist.

"Cobra."

He'd found it in the garden. The snake was a metre and a half long. Jorge was lean and bald and calm, and he used his hands with the precision of a craftsman. He wasn't squeamish with the snake; he laid it out on a plank like a salmon, chopped it into chunks, then, leaving aside the head, gathered the bloody meat and dropped it over the stone wall at the back for the pigs. We watched them snort and squeal and gorge. Jorge laughed gently through his nose.

"Pigs."

I'd met the pigs earlier that day while going about my business in the outhouse. Hearing noises, I'd looked down between my feet through the hole in the floor and saw the pigs jostling for position, pink snouts twitching, gazing expectantly upward.

Jorge and I watched the pigs polish off the snake, then turned our attention to some boys playing soccer out on the weedy grass.

Jorge, a man of few words, said, "Boys."

The other side of the house was all palms, fragrant flowers, and vegetables. Jorge lugged buckets of water to them. I followed him, fitting my footsteps to his, thinking of that cobra.

"You find a lot of snakes?"

He laughed that laugh. "Maybe two or three a year. The dogs keep them off."

The dogs, I noticed, were asleep in the shade.

Jorge looked up into a palm tree and pointed. "But is something there. Coming at night. I don't know what. Like mongoose. But big." He held his hands a metre apart.

A tiled porch inlaid with rose patterns traced the front and sides of the house. Jorge said his father built the place in 1937, then a year later died of "the sickness of the big belly."

One of Jorge's brothers lived in Lisbon. Jorge had gone there with him but hadn't lasted. He'd found the Portuguese reserved and suspicious, Lisbon crowded and cold compared to Goa, so he'd returned after two years.

❉

Ramone Rodrigues lived across the road from Jorge and Clementina Mesquita. He lived with his wife, son, mother, and sister. I got to know them. Ramone was a civil engineer and had been out of work three years. Fortunately, his father and brother had been working in Bahrain for the past decade and sent money. Their house was a monsoon-rotted hulk of cracked masonry and termite-riddled pillars, with branches for rafters. Every other day a roof tile dropped through and shattered on the floor. They claimed the house was two hundred years old. I would have said three hundred.

When I'd first arrived in Goa, Ramone's sister, Monica, had shown me a room they had for rent. She'd turned the rusted black lock with one of those classic old keys. I'd stepped in and looked around: dirt floor, stained mattress, no windows, a wormholed Christ on a crate, and an army blanket of cobweb sagging from the ceiling. They'd wanted a dollar a night. I'd liked that. But the room was too grotty even for me. I'd made excuses, smiled and shrugged, and said I'd be back. I'd crossed the street, where I'd found the room in the Mesquita's house. Still, I ate all my meals at the Rodrigues's, trying, in my small way, to spread the wealth. The Rodrigues didn't have the means to upgrade their house, much less send Monica to university. Ramone, with his big smile and a cruci fix tattooed along the inside of his forearm, enjoyed his enforced leisure. He hung out with his friends while Monica served food on the porch to young tourists on the cheap.

When Monica saw that I was renting a room at the Mesquita's, she confronted me. "You no like our room?"

I scrambled for an excuse. "It's a bit small."

"What you need so much room for? You little man."

At twenty-five, Monica was an old maid by Goan standards. When she wasn't making fruit salads or Nescafé for the travellers lounging about the porch in Muslim skullcaps and Rajastani vests, Monica leaned in the doorway of the old house, staring sullenly at the aluminum sky. That was her pose when I first walked up the dirt path seeking a place to stay. As I approached, a rat dashed out of the house, past her feet, and down the steps right past me into the garden. By then I'd become somewhat of an expert in rats. This one looked sturdy and rural and well fed. Monica didn't blink.

Although she would often prove to be sullen, I immediately discovered her dry humour. As I climbed the steps, she demanded, "What do you want?"

I don't know what possessed me, perhaps fatigue from the bus journey from Poona, but I answered, "I want thirty cups of Nescafé. No sugar."

She didn't miss a beat. "No sugar?"

"No sugar."

"Sorry. Only have twenty cup Nescafé no sugar."

I liked her already. Thick black hair, large dark eyes, defiant jaw. She wore a well-scrubbed white frock and thin-soled thongs.

She contemplated me. "What is your good name?"

My "good" name? I more than liked her, I was charmed.

Unlike her sister-in-law, who had already settled into the routine certainty of middle age and motherhood, Monica was tense and moody. One afternoon two of her friends arrived, each on her own motorscooter and laughing as they glided up the path. Monica smiled tightly. For the next hour the women posed on the porch, languidly fanned themselves, and complained alternately about their jobs as schoolteachers and about their husbands. After they left, Monica disappeared, and I didn't see her again until evening, when once again she stood in the doorway, arms folded.

"What are you thinking?"

"Not thinking."

"No?"

"Too old to think."

"You're twenty-five."

"Young body, old heart."

I asked about her friends.

She sneered. "These girls always talk-talk." She tossed her hand, dismissing them. We watched the setting sun silhouette the palms and mangoes and listened to the rising hiss of cicadas.

I asked if she had a boyfriend.

She clucked her tongue and shook her head. "Goan girl not have boy. Stay fresh."

We watched the bats tumble in the dusk and said nothing for a long time.

A few days later Monica's mother, Ezelita, showed me an

ad in the local newspaper for a fast-food counter attendant in Margao, a few kilometres inland. The salary worked out to be the equivalent of forty US dollars a month. Ezelita asked me to write an application letter for Monica. I asked Monica if she wanted the job.

Ever sensitive and suspicious, she said, "You think is no good?"

I wanted to say she could do better. But could she? "That's up to you."

"I want."

I wrote. Ezelita got the letter typed by an old man who sat by the road with an ancient Remington. And so the wait began, and the anticipation mounted. Monica met the mailman each morning when he rode up on his bicycle. Her hopes were crushing to witness. I went over the letter in my mind. Had I done a good job? We'd all composed it, but I worried. Meanwhile, Monica, Ezelita, and sister-in-law Norma discussed the position. Would a uniform be provided? Would the job include lunch? How much could she save in a year? In two years? Could she save at all? Then one morning all three rode the bus into Margao and looked at the place.

When they returned, Ezelita lit up one of her Gold Flake cigarettes and declared, with sudden expertise, "Location is good."

Monica no longer stood in the doorway. She paced. A week passed. Two weeks. Given the legendarily inept Indian bureaucracy, I was surprised they anticipated any response at all. Some days Monica acted like the job was hers, other days she shrugged in defeat, still others she feigned indifference.

Then one morning Ezelita returned from town with the bad news. A man had got the job.

"A Hindu," she said. She felt no need to elaborate on the widely held view that Catholics were discriminated against. Monica said nothing. She returned to the doorway and resumed brooding. Ezelita had many theories besides Catholic-Hindu animosity as to why Monica was passed over, ranging from Monica's being too old, to living in a house that took in dirty hippies, to being the daughter of a known drunk. Ezelita's husband's drinking was the reason he had spent ten years in Bahrain and planned to stay there indefinitely.

I asked Monica about him. She said her aunts and uncles were all respectable, but not her father.

"Why?"

She shrugged and said, "All the fingers of the hand are not the same."

※

One Sunday I went with the Rodrigues family to church. It was tiny, whitewashed, and packed. All the men wore dark suits, their hair shiny and rank with coconut oil, while the elderly women wore black, the middle aged blue, and the girls white. The mass was celebrated in Latin, and the homily in Konkani. Standing, kneeling, sitting with all these da Costas, d'Souzas, Coutus, and da Silvas reminded me of a minor character named Harris in E.M. Forster's *A Passage to India*. He's the Nawab Bahadur's driver, and he's Eurasian. After a minor car accident, the Nawab, Miss Quested, and Ronny Heaslop are whisked away in another car that happens along. Harris, however, is left squatting Indian-style in the road in the dark. He's not European enough to merit a place in the car, yet he's not Indian either, so he asks the night "What about me?" I thought of Clementina Mesquita, not European enough for her sweetheart's family.

Richard Francis Burton visited Goa in 1847, and he had much to say regarding the results of intermarriage between Portuguese and Indians. "The Mestici, or mixed breed, composes the great mass of society at Goa . . . [and] it would be, we believe, difficult to find in Asia an uglier or more degraded looking race than that which we are now describing." Burton went further, suggesting that Portugal's Indian colonies lapsed so quickly into sloth and corruption because interbreeding resulted in a "softness or malformation of the brain." Ahead of his time in many ways, Burton was a man of his time in many others. For one thing, he misjudged the extent of intermarriage in Goa, which in fact was relatively slight after the first few decades of contact. The prevalence of Portuguese names reflected not the degree of intermarriage but the practise of adopting a European name when converting to Catholicism — the prudent move if one wanted to succeed socially and financially. By the time Burton was there in the mid-1800s, the degree of Portuguese blood in any Goan would have been slight indeed.

From what I could see, the Goans were a strikingly handsome people. If they were suffering from a "softness or malformation of the brain," they nonetheless enjoyed a higher standard of living than in the rest of India. The case of Monica Rodrigues was one of bad luck. She was bright, attractive, and spoke three languages, but she was fated to serve fruit salad to dirty hippies like me, stare at the sky, and talk all day with her mother and sister-in-law.

The three women talked endlessly. I assumed that, like

most small-town people, they knew everything about each other and their neighbours. They did, but strangely they didn't. Monica told me her mother had been born in the Congo. I thought this very peculiar, so I asked Ezelita.

"No. I born Tanganyika."

Her father had worked on a coffee plantation, though doing what she wasn't sure. They'd returned to Goa when Ezelita was eight. I asked her what it was like in Tanganyika. She said she didn't remember. While I found it surprising that Ezelita had no memories of the first eight years of her life, I couldn't comprehend how, for all their constant talk, Ezelita didn't know her father's job and Monica didn't know where her own mother had been born.

Finally, I asked, "What do you talk about all day?"

Leaning in the doorway, Monica smiled slyly. "You."

❋

I confess I'd been having thoughts about Monica. To me, she represented all that was exotic. She'd also been casting certain looks my way. These looks, along with probing questions from Ezelita, made it clear that they had plans for me. But, I wondered, was I just a walking rupee, a ticket to the West? Probably. As for my own ulterior motives, I saw Monica as a chance to escape the West. I could move in, take up the role of resident expatriate, learn Konkani, and become an old India hand. This sounded pretty good compared to my options in Canada, where I'd worked in a sawmill, in a mass-production bakery, in a hospital, on a construction site, and delivered advertising flyers. Why not a life of tropical ease? Instead of winter, there would be the monsoon. In February we'd celebrate carnival, just as they did in Brazil. What did it require other than the willingness to take the plunge?

Lying on my bed beneath those ghoulish white hands holding the curtain rod, I found myself recalling a month I once spent on Rarotonga in the Cook Islands. It was, by all the classic criteria of romantic escapism, paradise. There was a blue sky, a blue sea, warm winds. There were palm trees, friendly girls, and a pace slow enough to ease the most hectic heart. Yet after a month — after two weeks — I was so bored I was talking to the cockroaches. One morning in Goa, I said goodbye to Monica, walked down the road, caught the bus to Margao, and then took another bus to Bombay.

✸

Camoens's involvement with a Goan woman was of a different order than mine. Deprived even of the hope of ever seeing Catherine de Ataide again, he bought a woman in the slave market, made her his mistress, and, judging by a poem he wrote, fell in love with her.

> . . . Never a rose in garden set
> More lovely was,
> To my eyes entranced,
> Nor bird in the field
> Nor a star in the sky
> Is as radiant for me
> As is she I love.
> Features that have rivals none,
> Eyes in which I find repose —
> Black and languid are those eyes,

Which seek not death to deal.
A living light doth dwell therein,
Making her my sovereign, me her slave.

His infatuation with this woman, whom he called Luisa Barbara, earned him ridicule. He rode it out. In this he was likely supported by the friendship he developed with two men, Diogo do Couto and Garcia da Orta. Both were educated and appreciated Camoens's poetic genius. Couto, nineteen years younger, was already writing a history of Portugal's colonial exploits. Orta, thirty-four years older, was a bibliophile, physician, and herbalist. It was now 1563, Camoens was thirty-nine years old, and he had spent ten years in the East. Both he and Couto spent a lot of time with Orta, who had a luxurious house filled with books and female servants. Like Camoens, Orta had also fallen in love with a slave, Antonia. Like both Couto and Camoens, Orta was also completing a huge literary work, his on the drugs of India.

Although well occupied during this time, Camoens was not content. He had a minor government job with no possibility of advancement. He couldn't save any money, and he was surrounded by ongoing examples of Portuguese barbarism, the worst of which was the Inquisition. To top it off, he feared that his poem, *The Lusiads*, would vanish unpublished and unread. So, in 1567, at the age of forty-three, he decided to return to Portugal — without Luisa Barbara.

THREE

Camoens's decision to return to Portugal proved easier than actually getting there. During the first years of Portuguese rule in India, captains had given free passage home to soldiers who had completed their terms of service. Now captains, and even the crew, rented out their cabins and hammocks to the highest bidder. Camoens didn't have any money. He'd been away from his homeland some fourteen years, and it looked as if he might spend many more yet. He got a break when one Pedro Barreto Rolim, recently appointed to the captaincy of Sofala, was about to embark for his new position. He hired Camoens to keep the ship's books in exchange for free food and passage as far as Mozambique. Camoens left no letter or record of how he felt saying goodbye to Luisa Barbara. Perhaps she'd been expecting it all along. I wonder if, in her old age, she thought of him at all, and if so with fondness or as just another erratic foreigner, lean, intense, always scribbling?

As for Camoens, after a fifty-day voyage, he found himself on the muddy, malarial shores of east Africa. But he was still broke. He was reduced to menial jobs, charity, and, perhaps worst of all, waiting and uncertainty. Homeward-bound ships were infrequent. When they did anchor offshore, the captains would have nothing to do with him. Although he was now geographically closer to Portugal, lacking money for his onward passage, he was, practically speaking, farther away. His fellow countrymen on land were only a few dozen illiterate soldiers. Camoens spent two years in Mozambique, two long years of waiting, watching for ships, trying to stay healthy, and, when he had the energy, looking over his poems. I imagine him in a hut, slapping mosquitoes, squinting one-eyed at his pages, reading his lines aloud as he revised them, then, exhausted, turning and staring at the horizon. Eventually, a galleon named Santa Clara *arrived. Aboard were Viceroy Dom Antao de Noronha and Camoens's friends Heitor da Silveira and Diogo do Couto. They got up a collection and paid Camoens's way. Still, the* Santa Clara *spent seven more months off Mozambique waiting for other ships from which it'd been separated during the voyage from Goa. Finally, it departed on its own.*

Shortly after they set sail, the viceroy died. He was buried at sea, except for his right arm, which he stated in his will was to be amputated at the elbow and taken to Ceuta and placed in the tomb of his nephew. So the Santa Clara *proceeded down the east coast of Africa, around the cape, and then northward, carrying one of Portugal's greatest historians, Diogo do Couto, its greatest poet, Luis de Camoens, and the forearm of a viceroy.*

BOMBAY 1998

In the years following 1990, I began to realize I had to go back to India and fill the holes in my research. I'd hardly glanced at Old Goa, and I'd missed Cochin altogether. So, eight years later, in November 1998, I flew to Bombay.

Bombay was now officially Mumbai. The latest maps and brochures called it Mumbai, and if you looked Bombay up in the index of a guidebook it was to Mumbai that you were scoldingly referred. Yet there was confusion. On the flight, for instance, the Singapore Airlines pilot kept mixing up the names, calling Mumbai Mombee, Bumbo, and Bumboy. In my mind, however, Mumbai would remain Bombay for a few more decades at least. The name Bombay carried too many associations to be so easily dumped. I felt far too much regressive and irrational romance for the largely mythic, but powerfully seductive, "exotic East," of which Bombay was an intrinsic part. In the years between this visit and my previous one, I'd read Edward Said's *Orientalism*, in which he deconstructs the concept of the Orient, laying it bare as the product of paranoid Europeans trying to define, reduce, and control the Other. He makes a convincing, if shrill, argument. But I didn't care. Bombay was Bombay.

Maybe it was punishment, but my first morning there I got hit on my bare toes with a gob of spit — not a mere spray of innocent white saliva — but a goober marbled with mucous. Hydrochloric acid could not have stung more. At that moment, if a surgeon had stepped up, I'd have begged for amputation.

The perpetrator, a bowlegged old woman, was already lost in the kelp-thick crowd. I limped back to the hotel and scrubbed my toes and my sandals in the sink with a bar of laundry soap.

The papers were reporting a resurgence of TB, yet everyone carried on hawking and spitting with a vile relish. Hygiene was losing the battle to habit. The practice of chewing betel nut encouraged spitting. It was common to see men who balanced brimming red mouthfuls of gob while talking and who sucked up the drool whenever it seeped down their chins.

I understood Arthur Koestler who visited India in 1958, comparing Bombay to an etching of a medieval town in the grip of the plague. But Bombay wasn't without fans. Dr. M.D. David, a local academic, opens his book *Bombay: The City of Dreams* with the grandiose generalization, "We all love Bombay." And Edward Lear, upon his arrival in India in 1873, gushed in his journal: "Extreme beauty of Bombay harbour! Violent and amazing delight at the wonderful variety of life and dress here. . . . O new palms! O flower! O creatures!" To that I could add "O the spitting!"

A greeny on your toe is not as bad as having to bludgeon a rat; still, it was not an auspicious start. So, to do something uplifting, something purifying on my first morning in Bombay, I decided to visit Mani Bhavan, the house once occupied by Mahatma Gandhi. This was across town, near the elite Malabar Hill district, where the Hanging Gardens were located, as well as the Towers of Silence on which the Parsis deposit their dead to be eaten by vultures. I caught a taxi. The driver was a hyperactive pervert from the southern state of Kerala, who, like a pornographic parrot, kept repeating

"Bombay good fucking! Bombay good fucking!" and gesturing obscenely with his thumb.

I told him I didn't want a whore.

"Good whores, Bombay. Good whores." And he gave me his most rakish wink in the rearview mirror.

"You'll get AIDS."

"No AIDS. Good fucking."

I tried diverting him onto another topic. "Is this taxi yours?"

"No. Driving only."

"How many days do you drive?"

"Every day."

"Seven days a week?"

"Yes."

"How many years?"

"Twenty-two."

"You've been driving every day for twenty-two years?"

"One day I had vacation."

"Only one day?"

"House exploded."

"Your house?"

"Many house. Boom!" He threw his hands up, letting the car steer itself.

At a red light, a man with no legs scooted out on a padded skateboard using two blocks to propel himself. I gave him a rupee. He smiled, showing immaculate white teeth and an excellent haircut. During my previous visits to India, I often considered choosing one beggar (on what basis I wasn't sure) and giving him or her a hundred dollars. My reasoning was

that this might be enough to get the individual set up in a business. At any rate, it might be enough to make the difference,
whereas passing out a few rupees here and a few rupees there
would only prolong the person's subservience. What a tale of
emancipation it would be, what a heartwarming story! In the
end I couldn't part with the hundred bucks.

We passed Chowpatty Beach, a Bombay landmark. Cow
Patty Beach would have been a more appropriate name. The
guidebooks all cautioned that it didn't look like much during
the day. And it didn't. In my experience, it wasn't much better
at night, when the acrobats and jugglers lounged indifferently
on the sand, the performing monkeys picked at their fleas, the
chained bears groaned, and the touts flogged hash and got
aggressive when you declined to buy some.

Rising above Chowpatty Beach, Malabar Hill was part of a
peninsula that extended into the Arabian Sea. As for the
Hanging Gardens, my notion that they had something to do
with the Hanging Gardens of Babylon proved completely erro-
neous. Situated atop a reservoir, the gardens were just that,
flower beds and trellises. It was a pleasant place to walk, the
highlight being a transvestite parading about in a sari. The
Indians found his prancing and primping hugely entertaining,
especially because he so badly needed a shave. The Towers of
Silence were next to the garden, a nondescript brick affair
strictly off-limits to non-Parsis. Disappointingly, there were no
vultures flapping off clutching limbs or skulls.

Following a map photocopied from a guidebook, I went
in search of Gandhi's house. As I was leaving the garden, a
balloon seller began dogging me. One of the balloons was

inflated to the size of a beanbag chair.

"How much?"

"One hundred rupees."

One hundred rupees was two and a half American dollars.

"For a balloon?"

"For packet. Ten piece."

I started walking away.

"Fifty!"

I continued walking.

"You don't like balloon?" he asked, implying "What kind of sour-spirited ogre could dislike balloons?"

"Sure, I like balloons."

"Only fifty rupees."

"But I don't want any."

"For children."

"I don't have any children."

"No children?"

"No."

He halted. "Because you are impotent bastard!" And with that he turned and headed back toward the garden entrance.

Mahatma Gandhi's house was on Laburnum Street, a quiet, affluent, tree-shaded road. The house was maintained now as a museum. Modelled scenes depicted the major events of his life, and his room, untouched, had the aura of a shrine. I stepped onto his balcony and imagined the great man in this same place, his feet perhaps right where mine were now. The trees would have been the same ones, and there would have been the same houses, maybe even the same old folks chatting in the shade below.

❁

That evening, walking back to my hotel, I passed my old haunt, the Leopold II Café and Bar. As usual, the place was packed with both Indians and foreigners. A voice beside me on the sidewalk enquired "You are an English gentleman?"

I turned to see a portly Indian walking beside me. He was about sixty, wore thick-framed glasses of black plastic, and had way white hair. "No."

"No?"

I gave him the sad news that I was merely Canadian.

"Ah, Canada. Very rich country. Toronto?"

"Vancouver."

"Ah. British Columbia. Your profession?"

I've never known how to answer that question. There was a time when I simultaneously went to school, worked in a bakery, and delivered advertising flyers. So what was my profession? If I said I was a janitor, as I'd been for awhile, people never believed me. How could a janitor — a sweeper — afford to travel? Teacher was the easiest response, despite the fact that I no longer taught. "Teacher."

"Subject?"

"Literature."

"Ah. Shakespeare, Shelley, Keats. I too am teaching literature." Then he became concerned. "I'm not bothering you, am I?"

I lied. "No, no."

"Good. I was just strolling. If I am bothering, I will leave."

Again I lied, "No problem." In fact, I was tired and just wanted to go back to the hotel and sleep.

"Would you be caring perhaps for some conversation?"

I looked about helplessly, as if to ask where on Earth we could possibly sit. The answer, of course, was the Leopold II.

"A beer," he continued. "A beer and some conversation. Ah." He slapped his ample paunch and observed, "Nothing like a beer in the evening."

I watched myself respond "Okay."

"So you are inviting me for a beer?"

No, I thought, you are inviting me to invite you, but I nodded nonetheless. Why not? He might be good for a laugh. Half a minute later we were seated in the Leopold II studying the beer list that sits under the glass-topped tables. To my horror, I watched him order the most expensive beer available, ninety rupees, over two U.S. dollars. For a guy like me, who once walked four hours from the Honolulu International Airport all the way to the youth hostel, rather than pay two dollars and fifty cents for the airporter, two bucks for a beer was too much. I'd stayed in some pretty good rat-free rooms for that price. How dare he order a two-dollar beer?

Fulfilling his side of the bargain, my new drinking partner launched into conversation, informing me that Canada had twenty-six million people and (repeating himself already) hinting that it was a very rich country.

"Oh yes, very rich." He was talking faster now, making with that left-right-left head wag without which Indians can't communicate. But I wasn't listening to his jabber. I was still brooding over the beer. I mean, why did he have to order the most expensive one? And a large bottle to boot? What came to me at that moment was not just the obvious suspicion that he was conning me but also the cliché about Canadians being so polite that they say thank you to the bank machine. Had I not been so polite, I'd have told the guy right up front "Yeah, you are bothering me." But the rule of politeness prevented that. After all, he was a portly, elderly gent who wore glasses. It all came down to that beer, though. If this was a con, he'd blown a sour note by ordering the most expensive brand. With the waiter right there — his pencil and pad poised to take my order — I leaned across the table and announced the not particularly brilliant conclusion "You're scamming me."

He rocked back as if I'd punched him. The shock! The insult! He stood. He stared. He swallowed hard. Then he whirled and walked out. Canadian politeness threatened to undo me again when, at the last second, I almost ran after him to apologize. Yet I managed to control myself. Nodding goodbye to the staring waiter, I slowly made my way to the door. I was halfway back to the hotel when I heard a voice raw with rage.

"And you call yourself a Canadian?" Trembling with rage, he stood in the street — the taxis and bicycles pushing past. I continued walking, and he began to follow me. "There he goes," he shouted, as if pointing me out in the hope of inciting the crowd to club me. "The Canadian bastard son of a bitch!" Then he wheeled and marched off the other way.

Maybe his dementia had something to do with Bombay's air. I don't mean the pollution, which, lit by headlights after dark, takes on an infernal quality, but its winds. These winds, observed the Victorian traveller Emma Roberts in the 1840s, "blow hot and cold at the same time." She noted that, "While enduring a very comfortable degree of heat, a puff of wind from the land or the sea will produce a sudden revulsion, and in these alternations the whole day will pass away, while at night they become still more dangerous to the mind."

By the time I got back to my room, my natural paranoia was whirling like a coked-up rat in a wheel. Was that slyly innocuous old gent the contact man in a gang preying on foreigners? Would he, in revenge, call the police and claim I'd tried selling him drugs? I worked out an explanation for when the police, accompanied by the hotel manager, banged at my door. My mind ran on, spinning ever more elaborate schemes, all of which ended with me in an Indian jail. Why hadn't I found out the name of the Canadian consul?

※

I woke to the cawing of crows. In the park across from the hotel, sweepers rearranged leaves, people took their constitutionals, children in uniforms ran to school. Even Bombay, predicted to be the most populated city on the planet by the year 2010, showed a freshness and innocence in the early morning. Skirting wide around the Leopold II, I went to VT station and reserved a second-class sleeper to Margao.

That night I returned to the station and waited for the Margao Express, scheduled to depart from track 11. I found track 11, studied the computer printout tacked to the reservations board, and there, in a feat of organizational efficiency by which Indian National Railways never failed to amaze me, found my name. I was in car S6, on bunk 46. And here was the Margao Express itself, rumbling slowly into position in all its groaning glory. It brought with it the smells of iron and grime and diesel oil. When it touched the bumper at the end of the track, I thought of an old bull with its forehead braced against a wall. The engine purged steam, and the smoke balled from its stack and drifted amid the iron-girdered ceiling. Passengers swarmed down the platform. I followed, looking for S6. I found S3, S4, S5 in a row but no S6. I kept walking. The crowd began to thin, and I thought, I'm going to run out of train. Then I spotted a chalk mark that could be interpreted as S6. I climbed in. They always stick the foreigners together, so when I found three dirty white faces I knew I was in the right place. There was a chain-smoking Cockney woman wearing blue polish on her finger- and toenails, a sullen Danish woman who would keep her hiking boots on all night, and a Russian guy of about forty.

The Cockney and the Russian were discussing suicide.

"Oi woudn' do it. Think uv me mum. She'd get it in 'er 'ed she'd fyled. Like as a parent an' all. Besides, oo'd look out for her after oi wuz gone?"

"Freezing is best," said the Russian, as if from personal experience. His name was Andrei. "You go to sleep, and then — " He shrugged as if that was that.

Contemplating death on an Indian train was not new to me. I'd nearly been killed on one fifteen years earlier, in October 1983. It was my second trip to India. The train, the 51 UP Sealdah Express, was en route from Calcutta to Pathankot. I'd already been on the train for thirty hours when the accident occurred. I was just settling in for my second night, stowing my shoes under my pack, which I used as a pillow, when the train crashed at a hundred kilometres an hour. I was on the top bunk, and a shudder ran the length of the cars. I began sitting up but found myself falling backward. In fact, the entire railcar was toppling, as if kicked over by a gigantic boot. We hit the ground with a massive slam. Then there was silence. A long silence, so it seemed, wherein we waited, motionless, wondering what had happened, where we were, and if anyone was hurt. The answer was a wail, a female voice rising out of the dark, followed, as if it was a signal, by other wails, and then we were all shouting, trapped in a railcar, or bogie, as they call them in India, groping about for packs and shoes and spectacles.

The train was upside down. After the initial panic subsided, I found myself crouched on the ceiling by one of the caged fans, looking out the barred window. It was midnight, and for some reason we'd crashed and toppled down the railway embankment into a fallow field. Gripping those window bars and staring out, I could see a man with a broken back. He'd been riding the roof, standard practice for Indian peasants, and when the bogies buckled he'd landed on the coupling. He would lie there draped across the coupling all night, moaning, unable to move, his spine a snapped stick. We couldn't get to him through the barred window and the aisle side of the compartment had collapsed, trapping us inside. They bar the windows in Indian trains to keep people from climbing in without paying.

Earlier that day at a station, I'd stepped off to get a bottle of water and had seen the people up on the roof in the sun. They appeared to be having such a great time that I considered climbing up myself. It looked better than our cramped and hot compartment. Although the second-class compartment was designed for eight passengers, up to twenty wedged their way in during the day. Only at night, when the bunks were dropped, did those without reserved seats reluctantly move off to stretch out on the floor or climb onto the roof.

There were six of us in the compartment. Two guys in their twenties, a grandfather and grandson, a Sikh sergeant, and me. The Sikh pried a plank from the floor, but it snapped when he tried it against the window bars. The compartment was full of dust and gravel. We were dirty and thirsty. The grandfather shared a bag of dates, but they only made us more thirsty. It was soon obvious there was nothing we could do, and soon there was nothing to say, so we sat there and listened to the goings-on outside. Along with the crying and shouting there was — bizarrely — laughter. We overheard two friends who had escaped unhurt.

"I lost my sock!"

"I lost some sleep!"

And off they went, giddy with relief.

At one point, a man clambered up the side of the bogie and stared in through the barred window as if at a zoo exhibit. He shouted something in Hindi. The others shouted back. He went away.

We settled in for the night amid the jumble of luggage. I'd like to say I spent that time wisely, reflecting upon the Eternal Questions. I didn't. But I did wonder about something, two things actually: the determination with which I'd worked to get on the train in the first place, and the fact that I was supposed to have got off an hour before the crash, at a town called

Ambala, where I'd planned to wait until morning and catch another train on to Simla. When we were nearing Ambala, however, I'd felt too tired to move. It was 11 p.m. Why get off now and sit in a station all night? I'd see Simla on my way back. So I'd paid the conductor another twenty-two rupees to continue on up the line and stayed right where I was in my by now familiar bunk. And then came that shudder rippling along the length of the train.

When I say I worked hard to get onto that train, I mean I spent two days trying to get the ticket. This was back in Bodgaya, the village where Gautama achieved his enlightenment and became the Buddha. It's a popular place with seekers and layabouts. Japan, Taiwan, Sri Lanka, Thailand, Tibet, and Burma maintain monasteries there. I had already spent those two months in the Buddhist monastery in Kathmandu four years previously, and now I'd done a month in the Burmese monastery pursuing my interest in meditation and the Buddhist philosophy of "bending like a reed in the wind." I realized that the Burmese monastery was also a great bargain, five rupees a night, which in 1983 was about fifty cents. That made my meditation upon the transitory nature of the material world much easier. If I was blowing big bucks, the thought of all that money disappearing would have made it impossible to concentrate and could have seriously hindered my spiritual growth.

A river ran past the Burmese monastery, and, each evening at sunset, men herded their bullocks into the water and washed them down. The cattle enjoyed it, wallowing in the water as the men and boys slapped and scrubbed each animal's muddy hide. It seemed a restful ritual. I felt sure the Buddha himself had watched the same thing.

But after a month I got bored with meditation and bullock washing and with the fact that the only restaurant in Bodgaya had mice-infested walls and lousy food. It was time to get moving, time to go up into the cool air of the mountains, to Dharamsala, home-in-exile of the Dalai Lama of Tibet. That meant getting a train ticket.

So I went to the station in Gaya, fourteen kilometres away. Gaya was as poor and as arid as any Indian town I'd ever seen, and Bihar, the name of the state, was feudal. I'd been told by an Indian engineer who owned a large tract of land in Bihar that, if a landowner wanted to deflower the bride of one of his tenant farmers, then he "jolly well did," and if the groom made any fuss he "got his bollocks lopped off."

At the train station in Gaya, I joined the line, an hour later reached the counter, and was told that there were no seats for six days. The Buddha, of course, would have gone with the flow, bought a ticket, and waited the six days in serenity. I tried. I bought the ticket and caught a jeepney back to Bodgaya and my room in the Burmese monastery. It was noon. At one I was pacing. At two I went back out to Gaya. I wanted to go — now! It was a familiar feeling, an unstoppable, irrational, impatience to move, to act, to run, and all the philosophy and Buddhistic blabber in the world was futile against it. Yet when I got back to the station, the ticket counter was closed. At four it reopened. Once again I waited in line, reached the counter, and this time flashed the clerk a hundred-rupee note. *Baksheesh*. Why hadn't I figured that out in the first place?

There were probably lots of seats. The clerk was an immaculately groomed guy with a pencil-thin moustache. He eyed the hundred-rupee note, eyed me, the note, then me again.

"I will give you advice. Tourist quota."

"Tourist quota?"

"Tourist quota."

I pushed the hundred-rupee note through the window in the grille. "Okay. Gimme one. For today."

He stashed the note. "Here we are not selling tourist quota. Central booking office you must go."

"Central booking office? Where's that?"

He gave me directions.

"And they'll give me a ticket?"

"Yes, yes."

"For today?"

He tipped his head left-right-left. "Of course."

I found the central booking office, which was manned by a prim young fellow who had a coleus plant potted in a Horlicks can sitting on his desk and a bicycle leaning against the wall beside him. "You have been misinformed. Station is selling." I returned to the station. The counter had closed, my hundred rupees were gone, and my train had already passed through.

I spent the following day going back and forth between the station and the central booking office, arguing with clerks, arguing with jeepney drivers, arguing with myself. But I wanted on that train. And the way to do it was to take action, to assert myself, to be, as they say, proactive. In the end I got my ticket, a second-class reserve sleeper, and late that afternoon I boarded the 51 UP Sealdah Express.

❋

Trapped with the others in the compartment, I did the only thing I could do, which was the very thing I hadn't wanted to do before — wait. The others were silent, and everything was surprisingly calm. Not even the discovery that my back was bleeding caused me much anxiety. I just sat there — shirt blood-stuck to my skin — and waited. I was lucky, I suppose. Since I'd been on the top bunk, so close to the ceiling, I hadn't been flung about. I was certainly luckier than the man with the broken back moaning just a few metres away on that iron coupling. And at least, being night, it was cool. Remembering the steam bath heat of the afternoon brought back memories of one of the passengers who'd shared the compartment earlier that day, a soldier for whom I'd developed a loathing. Not the Sikh sergeant here with us now but another guy. Things had been going all right until he showed up. At that point I was sharing the compartment with a family. The father was lean and cheerful, and his eyes alert. He smiled as he studied the people passing in the aisle. He also gave me part of their lunch, a red chili rolled in a chapati, which meant that for the rest of the day a coal burned in my belly and I burped fire. After lunch the tobacco and lime went around, and for the next half-hour mom, dad, auntie, and teenage son took turns gobbing out the barred window. The father's hands — lean, long, agile — made me think of precision tools. His wife, meanwhile, sat perfectly erect, eyes closed, as if meditating. The chatter rose and fell, alternately relaxed then animated. The teenage boy's arm encircled his younger brother's shoulders. Everyone was happy.

Then the soldier squeezed onto the bench directly opposite me. The family was impressed. They watched as he took off his shoes, peeled off his sticky socks, stripped down to his singlet, then propped his bare feet on the bench by my thighs. In India, to point your feet at someone is a grave insult. I pushed his feet away. He propped them back up. What, I wondered, would the Buddha do? Smile? Offer to rub the man's feet? I pushed them away again. We stared at each other. The soldier wiped his armpits with his shirt then held it to his nose. I asked him how it smelled. His response was a sneer. I checked my watch — another ten hours until Ambala. More people got on. The temperature rose. The fans continued to stir the sewagey air, and my thighs stayed stuck to the seat. Meanwhile, the soldier wiped out his armpits again then put the shirt to his face, as if savouring the smell of his maleness. He was a young guy, lean, lank-haired, and an industrious nose-picker. Averting my gaze, I studied the people standing chest to chest in the aisle, leaning on each other, sleeping, sweating, shouting, eating, smoking, spitting, and stinking of chopped onions. Once again I wondered what the Buddha would do. What I wanted to do was kill everyone or jump off and run screaming into the fields.

Somehow, though, the afternoon passed. The heat relented, and the sinking sun softened the Indian plain and filled the compartment with a silty light. And at long last the soldier got off. But not before a performance. As the guy pulled on his army shirt, the teenage boy, who'd questioned him closely all afternoon about military life, discovered an undone shoulder flap. Like an officer's aide, he was quick to do it up. The soldier took this as only natural. He pulled a mirror from his suitcase and handed it to his newfound assistant, who held it while the soldier arranged his matted hair. Discovering a blackened banana left over from his lunch, the soldier winked and, with all the bravura with which one can flourish a bruised banana, presented it to the youngest boy. A winning gesture! The family grinned in approval and wagged their heads left-right-left. And so it went, a bad actor drawing out his exeunt. When he was finally gone, the family launched into a discussion, confident that Mother India was in good hands. An hour later they too disembarked, others took their place, and we chugged on into the night. And crashed.

※

The eastern horizon was glowing like banked coals when a man pried the bars apart with an iron rod. One by one we climbed out onto the side of the bogey then jumped down. Fog dragged across the fields. I helped carry a man to what looked like an old bread van now serving as an ambulance. Sometime during the night, the man who'd landed on his back on the coupling had already been packed off. I joined the trek to the next station, a couple of kilometres along the tracks. The wreckage resembled a sacked city. Boys and men clambered in and out of the bogies shouting and laughing and looting. Another man, dressed completely in white, walked against the flow of people, weeping and talking to himself. His son, I learned, had been killed. The laughter slowed, then, when he had passed, picked up again.

The sun rose.

I reached the Gobindgarh Mandi station, a platform and a

shed, where Rotary Club members dipped up cups of chai from galvanized buckets and passed out cookies. I sat on my bag with my chai and cookie, the sun's horizontal rays easing my scraped and bruised back, and watched the kids romp as if the first snow of the year had fallen. A man whose face had grown youthful with relief heartily commended the prompt response of the Rotary Club and its most excellent chai. A reporter ducked about snapping photographs. The mourners, meanwhile, all sat apart in a moaning mass, as if their misfortune were a communicable disease. Later that day, the *Times of India* would state that sixteen people had been killed and 133 injured when the 51 UP Sealdah Express derailed.

Why had it derailed? I met a young Nepalese monk who had a theory. Glancing about for eavesdroppers, he whispered "The Muslims." He gazed at me, dark-eyed and dramatic. I didn't react. He perceived more fuel was needed. "They are an underhanded people."

His name was Thupten (the equivalent of Bob or John for Tibetans), and he was wrong about the train wreck. The *Times of India* said the derailment had been caused by Sikh extremists agitating for an independent Sikh state called Khalistan. They'd removed a section of the rail. Columnist Kushwant Singh wrote that the aim of the terrorists was to frighten Hindus out of the Punjab and draw Sikhs into it, thereby creating a de facto Khalistan.

A taxi bumped slowly past with a corpse wrapped in sheets tied to the roof rack. A boy on a bike chased the car ringing his bell. Thupten and I walked into the town and got a bowl of *dhal*. He was about twenty, on his way to Dharamsala to teach

English at the Tibetan centre and be near the Dalai Lama. Thinking about my determination to get on that train, and then paying extra to stay on, I asked him whether Buddhists believed in fate. He began talking about karma.

"You can influence karma by right action."

"Right action?"

He quoted an example from the life of the Buddha. "The Buddha," said Thupten, "once came to a bridge over a deep gorge. Twenty people were walking across this bridge. But as the Buddha approached, he saw a man on the far side who was about to cut the rope and send those people plunging to their deaths. So the Buddha picked up a stone and threw it and killed the man. The reason was this: he understood that the bad karma attached to the murder of twenty people would keep that man in the hell realms for so long that he'd never have the opportunity to rebuild his good karma with good acts. The Buddha, on the other hand, would suffer the bad karma attached to only one murder. From this he would quickly bounce back due to his other good acts, which now included the saving of those twenty people on the bridge."

At the end of this story, Thupten seemed very satisfied with the logic of the Buddha's action. We returned to the station. Soon another train appeared. By the time it rolled into the station, however, its two bogies had already been mobbed by passengers who'd run out to meet it.

I was in no mood to fight my way onto any more trains. I would wait. Hell, I'd walk. "Forget it," I said. "We'll never get on."

But Thupten was not about to be so passive. He wedged

himself up and into the car. A moment later, a compartment emptied. He waved me up, and suddenly I had a window seat.

"What happened?"

Thupten looked at me with great seriousness. "Peasant people. Very ignorant. I told them they were on the wrong train."

❈

Now, fifteen years later, in 1998, I was on another Indian train, this one from Bombay to Margao. I asked Andrei the morbid Russian if he'd flown Aeroflot from Moscow.

He nodded in disgust. "Is worst airline in world."

I told him how, in 1983, I'd flown from Delhi to Rome on Aeroflot.

"Then you have death wish."

No, I was just cheap. Aeroflot offered the best deal to Rome, and it went via Moscow. As I recall, the passengers were mostly Indian. Ever sensitive to cultural idiosyncrasies, the airline provided a meal dominated by sliced ham and sliced beef. It may as well have been carrion. The Muslims and Hindus sat as far back in their seats as possible and waved pleadingly to the stewardesses for the trays to be taken away. The Europeans, meanwhile, gorged. I'd planned it so that I'd have to overnight in Moscow — at the airline's expense — and get to go into the city. It didn't work out. First of all, customs took five hours. Then we were herded, at gunpoint, through calf-deep snow into a bus, driven two hundred metres to a hotel, and herded inside, and that was that. My room was on the fourth floor, and I shared it with an American engineer from Texas who'd been working in Siberia and who was now heading home. He liked Russia a lot. He especially liked Russian women. Stretching out on his bed wearing cowboy boots, he crossed his ankles. "Horniest goddamn broads you ever seen."

The hotel window looked out upon a snowbound birch forest. It was peaceful, if bleak. Most impressive of all, though, was that just twelve hours before I'd been in the glare and heat of India, four thousand kilometres southeast. Now I was in the USSR, in the snow. The next day, we were herded back out to the bus, driven two hundred metres, and herded into the airport. So much for my visit to Russia.

When I finished telling Andrei about my Russian adventure, he had only one thing to say: "Aerofart." Along with the Cockney and the Dane, Andrei was heading for Calangute, a beach in Goa known for its raves. I thought that if anything would keep me away from a beach, raves were it. So I was the only foreigner to stay on the train until we reached Margao, the last stop.

There were taxis, trishaws, and men on motorcycles waiting outside the station, all offering rides out to Colva or Benaulim beach. Now came the old dilemma. Motorcycle would be the cheapest, but climbing onto the back of a bike with a pack and plunging into the Indian traffic worried me. A taxi would be the safest but also the most expensive. I opted for a trishaw, cheaper than a taxi and safer than a motorcycle. Trishaws are three-wheeled motorcycles fitted with canopied wagons. The driver wanted seventy rupees, less than the price of that notorious beer in Bombay. Nonetheless, I bargained. A principle, after all, was a principle. When the driver wouldn't budge, I went to another trishaw. Its driver wanted the same

Husking rice, Benaulim (Goa)

amount. I smelled conspiracy. I considered walking. It would take me about three hours. I was stuck, and the drivers all knew it. Finally, I got in, said, "Colva," and we were off, weaving between puddles of reddish-brown rainwater.

I'd often imagined my return to Margao as a reunion. I had it all worked out. I'd stay with the Mesquitas in that room with the carved white hands sticking out of the wall, and each morning I'd cross the road and eat fruit salad with the Rodrigueses. As for resuscitating my fantasies about going Native and marrying Monica, that was out of the question. I was happily engaged to a woman back home. Besides, eight years had passed, and I knew myself better — not well, perhaps, but better. I didn't want to live in India. Yet, now that I was actually here in Margao, I got timid about visiting the Rodrigueses. I tapped the trishaw driver on the shoulder and said "Benaulim."

"No Colva?"

"No. Benaulim."

Benaulim was the next beach south, about seven kilometres from Colva. The area was all rice paddies, palm trees, and guesthouses. The trishaw dropped me at Maria Hall, a jungle-draped chapel at a crossroads. I declined offers from drivers of other taxis, trishaws, and motorcycles and started walking along a narrow strip of pebbly tarmac. On either side, aging bungalows squatted beneath palm and banyan and mango trees. The bungalows had deep verandas with cool stone benches shaded by tiled roofs. There were also many bright new cement buildings. Children, chickens, and pigs criss-crossed the road, women hung laundry on lines, men tinkered with motors. The sea was over a kilometre away, but I could smell the salt. Foreigners strolled about in beach wear, sand sticking to their oiled legs. I found a room in a hotel that, while lacking the character of an older Portuguese-style bungalow, was clean and cost only $4.50 U.S. a night.

As far as I could tell, I was the only guest. In the backyard, the owner's wife, Isabel, was scuffling back and forth through a dozen square metres of rice. The rice was spread out on a mat, and Isabel, barefoot, wearing a white frock, was husking it by walking on it. Out front, a line of water buffalo was ambling past along a muddy ridge that divided two paddies. White birds rode on their backs. Directly above, hawks floated in the hot air. Palm trees, rice paddies, blue sky. Paradise. Now what? Head down to the beach for a swim in the Arabian Sea? No. Sleep? No. I found myself heading for Colva. I had to say hello to the Rodrigueses.

It seemed a longer walk than I remembered, especially in the heat. I looked for familiar landmarks but didn't recognize any. The Rodrigueses lived on a narrow road about a kilometre back from the beach. Yet the road looked older and narrower, the shop I'd frequented more rundown, and when I neared their house I didn't recognize it. Becoming wary, I decided just to pass by and take a peek, maybe not go in at all. Despite the building boom under way, this side of Colva had been forgotten, and the bungalows appeared shrunken and overgrown. The guidebook gave only the vague statement that there were various family-run places along here. It soon became obvious why the book devoted so little space to the Rodrigues and Mesquita homes. Both buildings looked condemned.

Despite the weather-beaten board advertising that rooms were available (pleading seemed more appropriate), the Casa Mesquita looked derelict. Over the centre of the Mesquita's balcony, directly in front of the entrance, hung a blue tarp. The potted plants that had lined the ledge were gone. Everything seemed smaller and darker, even the plants. There was my old room. From the street it looked like a cavern. How could any light have penetrated those windows? I walked past, crossed the road, then came back and looked at the Rodrigues house. The rosebushes and garden tables had been replaced by a square cement building painted blue. Inside, six locals were drinking beer and playing cards. I looked at the house, and at the balcony on which I'd had so many meals and conversations. Taking a big breath, I stepped in off the road toward the house. A woman I recognized as Monica's sister-in-law, Norma, trotted down the steps waving me back as though I was an intruder.

"Yes? What you want?"

I remembered my first conversation with Monica. I tried to think of something witty to say. I failed. "Do you have drinks?"

"Dring? You wan' dring?" She gestured me away from the house and toward the blue concrete box. I stepped in and nodded to the card players. Even as concrete boxes went, this one struck me as pretty sad. A couple of tables, a cooler containing bottles of Kingfisher beer and orange pop, and a door leading to a dim room at one end.

Then Ezelita appeared. She'd shrunk. She'd seemed so solid eight years ago; now she looked deflated. Her thongs were thin, and she'd lost a couple of upper teeth. But she had

A girl in South India (Kerala)

her pack of Gold Flake cigarettes and her Cheeta brand of wooden matches. And she was eyeing me with something more than curiosity, despite the fact that I no longer wore a beard (it had gone a little too grey for comfort). So, in the afternoon heat, we studied each other but, as if wary, said nothing. I reminded myself of the number of foreigners she must see each year. As it turned out, there hadn't been all that many. In fact, judging by the looks of things, hardly any at all. Ezelita called to one of the card players, a lean, balding man of about thirty-five with a thick moustache. He was drunk, but he got an orange pop for me, opened it, and even managed, after a few tries, to slot a straw into it. The carbonation, however, insisted on popping the straw back out. This exercised the drunk's mind. He frowned as if at an engineering problem. He grabbed the straw, mangling it, and concentrated on ramming it down with his thumb while Ezelita and I watched. Finally, he passed it to me, his palm lidding the bottle as if there was a bee in it. I drank half, then announced, "I stayed here once."

This revived Ezelita. "Here?"

"Across the road. At the Casa Mesquita. But I ate here. Every day. For a month."

Now she resumed studying me and slowly began nodding her head in recognition.

"I had a beard."

"Eight year ago?"

"In February."

"Febwary?"

"You asked me about Valentine's Day."

"Walentine?" She lit a cigarette and turned to the drunk and spoke to him in Konkani. The drunk towed a blue plastic chair over and sat on it. "This my son. He in Gulf eight year ago."

Somewhat more sober now, he nodded at this. "Bahrain."

I recalled that Ezelita's husband had been working in Bahrain. "Doing what?"

He raised his hands and held an invisible steering wheel. "Drive bus."

"You will stay to Christmas?" asked Ezelita.

I thought that was unlikely. "No."

"Where you stay?"

"Benaulim."

"Benaulim?"

"Yes."

She nodded and smoked.

I looked around. "Where are all the tourists? It used to be so busy here."

She lowered her cigarette and looked at me. "Benaulim."

I felt a flush of guilt. "There are lots of new hotels there."

"Yes. New hotel."

There was a silence. Finally, I asked, "Your daughter. Monica. Is she still here?"

She hesitated. "Monica?"

"Yes."

"She go out."

"Margao?"

"Yes. Margao."

But I could see that Ezelita was hiding something. If

Monica was married, she'd be living with her husband, and Ezelita would simply come out with it. So I eliminated marriage. I wanted to ask other questions but felt awkward. Who was I, some stranger, prying for details about her family? We sat on in silence, the card game continuing at the other table. "What about Ramone? Your other son. The one with the tattoo." I extended my forearm. "Of a crucifix."

"Crucifik?"

"Yes."

"No crucifik."

"No?"

She shook her head.

I was absolutely certain Ramone had a crucifix tattooed along the inside of his forearm. Beginning to doubt my own memories, I turned to the son sitting with us now. "Did you like Bahrain?"

"So hot."

"Hotter than here?"

"Hot-hot."

Ezelita nodded profoundly. "Yes, Gulf wery hot."

We talked a little more, and then, deciding to return in a few days, I said goodbye.

Ezelita said, "Okay."

❋

I left the Rodrigues's feeling disappointed and saddened. Still, I hadn't gone all the way back to Goa just to visit them but to find out more about the attitude of colonial nostalgia so strong among Catholic Goans. There wasn't a lot of information available on the departure of the Portuguese, and what was seemed biased one way or the other. The liberation was framed as either a glorious event or an invasion. I'd done a lot of research at the University of British Columbia library and picked up P.D. Gaitonde's *The Liberation of Goa: A Participant's View of History*. On the title page, handwritten block letters announced "THIS BOOK IS ONE-SIDED IN FAVOUR OF INDIA." Another book consisted totally of letters and testimonials written against India's military action in Goa. For his part, Gaitonde chronicles the entire history of the Goan liberation movement. He notes how the Hindus, who comprised two-thirds of the Goan population, were discriminated against "on the grounds that they did not profess the state religion" of Roman Catholicism and that, "as late as 1907, Hindus were not allowed to teach in Portuguese primary schools."

According to the Catholic Goans I spoke to, however, the situation seemed to have reversed itself. Every Catholic Goan complained that they were excluded from jobs and that the quality of life had declined; every Hindu Goan claimed that life had improved. Inacio Fernandes was a Catholic. He owned the hotel I was staying in, plus a new Japanese car, and was doing very well indeed. He was even getting a new electric sign for his establishment. But he was not optimistic.

"The problem is, we Goans do not know how to bribe."

"No?"

"Of course not." He appeared insulted that I should be so ignorant of the moral calibre of the Catholic Goan. "Because, you see, in Portuguese time the bureaucracy, the government, it worked. Goans got jobs if they were qualified," said Inacio.

"You apply — you get. But now that is not the way. Now you must. . . ." He rubbed his thumb and forefinger together, meaning bribe. "The Indians understand this, but the Goans don't."

Inacio was about fifty, five-foot-five, had wavy hair and a comfortable paunch. He was amiable with the guests, stern with his employees, and kind to his Doberman, Tipu Sultan. He tipped his head to one side and gazed sadly at me. The message in his large dark eyes was that the Goans — modern and European — had been thrown to the Asian jackals. They were too ethical for a system as corrupt as that of Hindu India.

We got onto the subject of Bal Thackeray, leader of the Shiv Sena, the Army of Shiva, an aggressive Hindu nationalist party. As well as being lampooned by Salman Rushdie, Thackeray has been called a Hindu Hitler and a fascist.

"Him." Inacio sat back as if avoiding a stench. "Divide and rule. He is practising divide and rule. Driving a wedge between the Catholics and Hindus."

Hindu nationalism had Christians, and especially Muslims, worried. And for good reason. The Ayodhya incident was in the news again. In 1990, in the town of Ayodhya, enraged Hindus had torn down a mosque believed to be built on the site of an ancient Hindu temple. Now two Hindu brothers, the Kotharis, killed by police during the riots, had just been proclaimed martyrs for having, in the words of Uttar Pradesh Urban Development Minister Lalji Tandon, "sacrificed their lives for the construction of the *Ram mandir* at Ayodhya." In their honour, a granite-and-marble memorial had been raised.

Just a week earlier, the November 16, 1998, issue of the magazine *India Today*, included an article on the Kotharis, remarking upon "the Centre's subtle attempt to Indianise and nationalise" the educational system. Textbooks were being prepared "with the aim of inculcating Hindu religious consciousness and pride among school children." One text reportedly contained a chapter titled "The Martyrs of November 2," referring to the Kotharis. The Uttar Pradesh state government also planned to introduce the recitation of the Hindu prayers Saraswati Vandana and Cande Mataram in government-run primary and junior high schools. Critics insisted that the very fact that these prayers were not to be compulsory in minority schools would only encourage minorities to drift into segregation and thereby cause marginalization, isolation, and suspicion.

"Divide and rule," repeated Inacio. "In the Portuguese time no one knew who was Hindu and who was Catholic."

Behind him, the gardener and cook nodded in agreement with the man who paid their wages.

Gaitonde maintained that Hindus and Catholics have known who was who ever since the days of the Inquisition. An edict of the Inquisition, published in 1736, stated that "Goan Christians should, in all their behaviour, lose all resemblance to the Hindus and conform to that of the Portuguese from whom they receive the incomparable gift of conversion." To Gaitonde, liberation was an attempt to undo this enforced division and reunite Goans with their brethren in the neighbouring state of Maharashtra.

In 1963, the Maharashtrawadi Gomantak party, "dedicated to the immediate merger of Goa with the adjoining State of Maharashtra," won the state elections. Gaitonde interpreted this as meaning that "the majority opinion did not regard Goa as a separate cultural entity." By 1967, however, that view had changed. A poll showed that not just the residents of the Velhas Conquistas but also the entire state was now in favour of remaining separate, as a Union Territory. Gaitonde suggested that this change of opinion on the part of the Hindu majority was due to economic advantages to be had if Goa remained a discrete administrative unit.

※

The day after visiting the Rodrigueses, I took the bus to Panjim, the capital of Goa, fifty kilometres north of Margao. The bus was painted with Catholic saints and sayings. The glass separating the driver from the passengers showed Mother Teresa praying to Jesus Christ's head (which looked like a moose head mounted on a board). The ride from Margao to Panjim took an hour, and the road passed whitewashed churches, memorials, and many new and affluent-looking houses sporting names such as d'Souza Mansions and Mirador Estate. In the Panjim bus station, I met a sixtyish man named Kamat. He was short and fragile-looking and carried a briefcase. I wanted to mail some letters, so I asked him for directions to the post office. It was right on his way, so we walked together.

As usual, his first question was "What is your country?"

"Canada."

"Ah." He was pleased. I'd given him an opportunity to reminisce. "This reminds me of an anecdote." And he proceeded to tell me about his days as a financial adviser in Chandigarh, in the Punjab. Apparently, a Sikh living in

Canada wanted to return to India. "I advised him on how best to protect the money he'd made abroad. He is so pleased with my counsel that he tells me, 'Kamat, you and your wife will come and visit me for one month in my home.'"

"Did you?"

"Ah. That is the conclusion to which I am leading." As we crossed the bridge into town, Kamat said, "In between times, I was transferred to Delhi. And then soon I am returned here to Goa. Contact was lost."

"So you never went?"

"I am still waiting."

"How long has it been?"

"Eleven years."

Kamat was a Goan-born Hindu. He'd have been about twenty when the Portuguese left. I asked him if he spoke Portuguese, and he said he'd studied it until the third form, about the equivalent of grade nine in the North American school system.

"Has Goa improved since liberation?"

"Oh my God, yes."

"How?"

"Development. So much development." He gestured as if one need only look around for proof.

I confess I didn't see much. Panjim was a pleasant enough city by Indian standards, due mostly to its small size, though the dominant impression was not of development but of decay.

"Literacy has risen to eighty percent," said Kamat. "There is infrastructure." He placed his hand upon my forearm as if to console me. "Of course, here in India we are the cradle of civilization. We were playing chess and inventing astronomy while you Europeans were living in the trees."

Living in trees. I'd heard this phrase before in various places from various mouths. Yes, you Westerners may be running the show now, but where were you a thousand years ago? Even Westerners, abasing themselves in guilt at the accomplishments of their parents and the affluence they themselves had inherited, announced that, Yes, while you in the East had a great culture, we in the West were living in trees and scratching our bums.

I thought of Puri, a beach town on the east coast where a woman named Gita and I became enemies because I punched a cow. India's wandering cows are generally inoffensive and occasionally endearing. But on this particular morning I spotted a cow eating my Levis. I'd just washed them and hung them on a rope strung between two beach pines. The cow had wandered into the yard behind the hotel and decided, Oh ho! Breakfast! I was sitting on the porch eating my own breakfast when I discovered what the cow was up to. I ran down the steps, grabbed what remained of my Levis, and pulled. The cow clenched its teeth. So I punched her, right on that big pad of muscle at the base of the jaw. She let go, and I hauled my jeans up. They looked like they'd been caught in a bicycle chain greased with slime.

At that point Gita ran down the stairs, wrapped her arms around the blandly unconcerned cow, and began yelling at me. "The cow is sacred. It's our mother. We don't hit our mothers."

According to the hotel manager, who'd seen her passport, Gita's real name was Phyllis Rosenberg. She was wrong.

Indians do hit cows. I'd seen it. They whack them, kick them, and punch them. It was the most effective way to stop a cow from eating your carefully constructed pyramid of oranges or to get one out of the intersection.

"These jeans cost me fifty bucks."

But Gita-Phyllis didn't care about my jeans. She stomped back up to the breakfast table on the porch, returned with her fruit salad, and began feeding the cow.

"What you don't understand," said Gita-Phyllis, "is that we had a great civilization when you Europeans were still living in the trees."

Gita apparently believed herself to have been an Indian in a previous life. "What about the Greeks?" I said.

"The Greeks weren't European, they were Mediterranean."

"The Romans?"

"So were they."

"Then where was Europe?"

"Germany. Germans were wearing ox horns on their heads and eating raw meat while we were inventing chess and astronomy."

❀

After posting my letters, I wandered past the Goa Medical College. Once a pale yellow, its walls were now stained black. The iron grilles over the windows were crusty with rust, and even as I stood looking a nurse poked a fist full of trash out an upper-floor window and let it flutter into the ruined garden. Yet Panjim retained a Mediterranean look in its tile-roofed bungalows with their shaded verandas and ornamented eaves. Other hints of its Portuguese past lingered. In the market, I was addressed as "Patrone." Then there were the Latin moustaches and sideburns of the older men, the women in frocks rather than saris, and of course the saints and cruci-fixes dangling from people's necks.

※

Although Panjim itself looked antique, Kamat was correct in saying there had been development. Tourism, brewing, and dis-tilling were vital to the state economy. These activities helped to replace the smuggling that had been so lucrative during colonial times, when Goa was a duty-free port and source of gold, whiskey, cars, electronics, and other European goods.

I wandered along the riverfront, where a few rusted freighters ploughed sluggishly up the Mandovi. Shipping was nothing new here. In the eleventh century, horses from Arabia were shipped inland to Vijayanagar, whose ruins now lay out-side the town of Hampi. When the Portuguese arrived in India, the Hindu king of Vijayanagar had recently been defeated by the sultan of Bijapur, a Muslim. The Portuguese took advantage of this in 1510 by helping the Hindus drive out the Muslims. With the Muslims gone, the Portuguese took over. Thus, they gained Goa and began establishing Portugal's Eastern empire. The capital, Old Goa, was soon described as the *Lisbon of the East*. I suspect the writer who coined the phrase was delirious with fever and scurvy, and giddy with relief after six or more months at sea. Still, Old Goa grew and by 1600 is said to have had a population larger than that of either London or Lisbon at the time. Some guidebooks put the figure as high as

300,000, but more likely it was about 75,000. It was known as both Golden Goa (Goa Dourado) and Queen of the East. A saying became popular that "He who has seen Goa need not see Lisbon." Even Goa's streets became known in Europe: Auction Road, Goldsmith's Road, Jew's Road. The first printing press in India was established in Old Goa in 1556.

Yet the city didn't last. Around 1700 a series of cholera and malaria epidemics devastated it. By the mid-1700s Old Goa was empty. The population had moved about ten kilometres upriver, where, in 1758, the Portuguese established a new capital, Panjim.

When Sir Richard Francis Burton visited Goa, he was unimpressed with either Old Goa or Panjim. In his typically droll fashion, he wrote that "Panjim loses much by close inspection." He went on to observe:

> *That Panjim is a Christian town appears instantly from the multitude and variety of the filthy feeding hogs that infest the streets . . . [which] are dusty and dirty. . . . The doors and window-frames of almost all the houses are painted green, and none but the very richest admit light through anything more civilized than [polished] oyster-shells.*

The only thing that impressed Burton about Goa was Camoens, so much so that Burton translated *The Lusiads*.

✿

After a few hours of wandering Panjim, I decided to head

upriver to Old Goa and spend the afternoon looking at the churches. The sky was partly overcast, and humidity hung like hot fog. Stepping into a store to buy a bottle of water for the trip, I met Joseph Pereira. He was watching a large new Toshiba television. Joseph was in his mid-fifties, fair-skinned, frail, goateed. The BBC *World Service* was reporting the hunger strike of the jailed terrorist Carlos the Jackal.

"What do you think of that?" I asked.

Pereira didn't take his eyes off the screen. "They should kill him."

"You think so?"

He looked at me. His black hair was lank with sweat, and he had a circular Band-Aid stuck to his temple. Rimless glasses magnified his eyes. "All those people he killed? Of course. But because he is famous he thinks he deserves privileges. It is like Bill Clinton."

"Oh?"

"Bill Clinton too thinks he deserves privileges. Okay. You do what you want. But he is public official. You cannot do these kinds of things." Joseph watched for my reaction.

I opted for the Indian gesture of maybe yes, maybe no, and tipped my head left-right-left.

"The Americans want to strike Iraq. Russia and China say no. UN says no. But the Americans don't care. They want to punish Saddam."

As Joseph talked, I realized that he thought I was American and was purposely provoking me. I let him continue. Again I offered the Indian maybe yes, maybe no. Behind Joseph, the shelves were stocked solid with Doctor's Choice Whiskey, Three Monks' Rum, Cashew Fenny, McDowell's Whiskey. Because I was offering no argument, and because I finally explained that I was Canadian, not American, he eventually began to relent. He raised his hand palm outward. "I am not against the American people. Only against American policy. And that policy is going to start World War III. It is as Nostradamus said. You know Nostradamus?"

"The seer."

"The Muslims are as one now thanks to the American policy. They are the Eastern foe Nostradamus predicted."

This wasn't the first reference I'd heard to Nostradamus here in Goa. Another fellow, out of work and with perhaps too much time on his hands, had explained to me that American aggression toward Iraq, global warming, and El Niño were all signs that, with the end of the millennium only fourteen months away, the end of the world was nigh.

"And now India has the bomb," I said.

"India!" It disgusted Joseph even more than America.

"You don't think you should have the bomb?"

He gazed at me with great dignity. "I am not Indian. I am Goan. Technically — technically — I am Indian. But culturally, historically, mentally," he tapped his temple above the Band-Aid, "I am Goan." Then he raised his right forefinger. "Four hundred and fifty-one years. Four hundred and fifty-one years we were a Portuguese colony." His voice became shrill. "An overseas state! We had equal citizenship to continental Portuguese. Until Salazar." Now Joseph wilted. "Okay. To be a

colony is to be inferior. But four hundred and fifty-one years."
He paused to let the figure sink in, then repeated it once more,
in case I'd failed to appreciate the dimensions of four and a
half centuries of colonial association. "Four hundred and fifty-
one years changes you," he said, as if he personally had
experienced every hour, day, and week of those years. Now he
pointed toward what I assumed was India. "We are different."

"But now you're free."

"Free." He reached for the remote control and reduced the
volume on the cricket report. "We went from Portuguese rule
to Indian rule."

Recalling Kamat, I said, "There's been development."

"There would have been development anyway. And there
was development before. The railway, the port, the mines." He
began counting on his fingers. "From Brazil the Portuguese
brought potatoes, chillies, tomatoes, cashews, pineapples!
What have the Indians done? Nothing. A bureaucracy so corrupt even they joke about it. This." He rubbed his thumb and
forefinger together in the same gesture Inacio had used. "This
is the only thing the Indian understands. The only thing that
gets anything done. With the Portuguese it was not like that.
There was law, there was order, there was no crime. And the
bureaucracy, it functioned. Look." He picked through a stack
of newspapers on top of the TV and slapped down a copy of
the Sunday *Navhind Times*, November 8, 1998. In it was an
interview with a one-hundred-year-old man described as "a
freedom fighter." I gave it a skim, expecting a damning account
of India. Instead, I found vague reminiscences. The freedom

fighter came across a bit muddled, as might be expected of anyone that old. He meandered from fond nostalgia for the old orderly days of the Portuguese to the opinion that "life is better today." He said that "Liberation of Goa — 1961 — was a wonderful event. There was jubilation all around. But soon disillusionment set in. I blame the politicians."

After skimming the article I nodded politely, not sure exactly what point Joseph was supporting with it. But by then he was on to another topic — Hindu nationalism.

"Nehru said our rights to distinct culture and identity would be respected. But Bal Thackeray and the Shiv Sena don't care. Okay. Look. In Portuguese era there were excesses. Torture even. I don't deny. But never did they try converting everyone. Thirty-five percent of Goa is Catholic. If they did try, then Goa would be hundred percent Catholic. Of the Hindu nationalists, you cannot say the same."

This was a line of argument I'd yet to hear.

Now Joseph asked, "You are Christian?"

"Technically."

"There are Goans in Canada?"

"A few."

"There is racial discrimination?"

"Lots."

His eyes opened wide behind his glasses. He launched into a lecture on blood. "All blood is the same. Black man, brown man, white man, yellow. The same."

I agreed, which meant Joseph had to move on to another topic. Nearby, an old woman was squatting on the sidewalk with a few bunches of bananas laid out on a sheet of news-paper.

"Look at her. You do not have this sort of thing in Canada."

When I told him that we did, Joseph was certain I was lying.

"But," he insisted, with a sort of perverse pride, "it is not as bad as here."

"No."

This seemed to satisfy him. "And Muslims, do you have Muslims in Canada?"

"Yes."

He drew himself up tall. An expression of distaste pinched his mouth. "The Muslims are the most filthy, underhanded people on the planet."

I glanced fearfully at the people passing on the sidewalk. One man's head spun, and his steps slowed. Joseph, if any-thing, drew himself up even taller yet remained adamant. My own experience of Muslims, in Morocco, Tunisia, and espe-cially Turkey, had been of almost obsessive hospitality and goodwill. Joseph did acknowledge, however, that Saddam Hussein was a brave warrior.

"He stands up to the Americans."

"And his blood is red," I added.

"We are equal," said Joseph as if reciting a proverb, "but we are not the same."

❋

From Panjim to Old Goa is about ten kilometres. To get there,

Coconut husking (Kerala)

I returned to the bus station and bargained for a trishaw. The driver, a Muslim, had a chinstrap beard and an embroidered skullcap. He wanted eighty rupees.

"That's too much."

He observed me with supreme indifference.

I walked away. When he failed to run after me grovelling for my business, I was forced to return and grovel for his services.

"Forty rupees."

His head staggered back in snorting laughter, revealing teeth as sharp and black as bat's ears.

"It's only ten kilometres."

"Petrol."

"Fifty."

He crossed his arms over his chest and took an interest in the sky.

"Sixty."

The sky continued to hold his interest.

"All right. Eighty."

I got in the back of his three-wheeled junker, and he kick-started it to life.

When we were under way, I began wondering about the Muslim view of life in Goa. I leaned forward and called over the racket, "So, Goa is good?"

His glance pinned mine in the rearview mirror, but he said nothing.

I said it again. "Goa is good?"

He tipped his head left-right-left.

I tried another angle. "Bill Clinton is a bastard."

"Beel Cleen-ton?"

"Yes."

He shrugged and drove on, saying nothing.

"Saddam."

"Saddam? Goddamn Saddam."

❊

Old Goa is now a World Heritage Site. There are no houses or shops or offices, just touts flogging plastic crucifixes, plastic rosaries, skinny candles, Saint Francis of Xavier postcards, and Thums Up Cola. One elderly man squatted behind a scale, on which, for a rupee, you could weigh yourself before visiting the elephantine churches and monasteries, relics of the bygone days of Roman Catholic rule.

Old Goa gave one dominant impression — that of authority. It was a city of churches and chapels and convents and monasteries, a city where, for two centuries, the Inquisition presided. Despite a large population of monks and priests — or perhaps because of it — Old Goa was also notorious for sloth and immorality. Slave owners functioned as pimps, idle soldiers mugged people, bored wives dosed their husbands with datura and, while the cuckolds lay unconscious, enjoyed their lovers in adjacent rooms. A Dutchman, John van Linschoten, visited Goa in 1583 and described this use of datura:

> *They haue likewise an Hearbe called Deutroa which beareth a seed, whereof bruising out the sap, they put it into a Cup or other vessell, and give it to their Husbands, either in meat or drinke, and presently therewith, the man is as though he were halfe out of*

*his wits, and without feeling, or else drunke, doing
nothing but laugh, and sometime it taketh him sleeping, whereby he lyeth more like a dead man, so that
in his presence they may doe what they will, and take
their pleasure with their friends, and the husband
neuer know of it.*

❉

I entered the Basilica of Bom Jesus to escape the heat. The
basilica housed the remains of Saint Francis of Xavier, the
apostle of the Indies and patron saint of Goa. Born in a castle
on the southern slopes of the Pyrenees in 1506 — the year
Columbus died — Xavier was handsome and athletic. He had
two great influences in his life. The first was his tutor from the
ages of ten to nineteen, Martin de Azpilcueta, who brought out
the scholar in Xavier. The second was Ignatius Loyola, who
brought out the missionary in him. Xavier and Loyola met at
university in Paris. Loyola was a penniless, thirty-six-year-old
soldier of fortune, Xavier a twenty-year-old dandy who liked
fine clothes and wine. Yet Loyola had a sense of purpose as
pointed and sharp as a sabre, and Xavier was captivated by
his passion to found a new order of knights sworn to the service of Christ. This would be the Jesuits.

The Jesuits were extreme from the start. Loyola guided
them through exercises of discipline, prayer, and self-mortifi-
cation. At least once Xavier became so enthusiastic that "With
hard and tightly bound strings he tied his arms and his legs so
that the flesh swelled and broke, and almost entirely covered
the cord." He never relaxed his principles of austerity and

poverty. When Xavier was about to depart for India, the king of Portugal sent a message stating that Xavier needed a personal servant. "Your position demands it. You cannot wash your own linen, nor busy yourself over the stock-pot." Xavier declined. He not only washed his own clothes and watched his own stock-pot, but he spent the voyage out to India washing and feeding the sick as well. He went to work immediately in Goa, baptizing so many in such a short time that he said "Often my arms are weary baptizing, and I cannot speak another word from having so repeatedly recited the prayers to the people one after another." He estimated that he baptized ten thousand people in one month. The figure is so absurd I think of the mass marriages performed by the Reverend Moon. Xavier was a guy who apparently lived to baptize and baptized to live. A veritable baptizing machine, he was known to climb trees and preach from the branches.

Xavier died in 1552, the year before Camoens's arrival in India. The story of the handling of Xavier's remains is as grisly as it is fascinating. In 1554, during the first public exhibition of Xavier's corpse, one Isabel de Caron, in a fit of reverence — or who knows, maybe hunger — bit off the fifth toe on the right foot. In 1614, the right arm, from the elbow down, was amputated and sent to Rome. In 1619, the remainder of the right arm was cut off, divided into three parts, and sent to the Jesuit Colleges of Malacca, Cochin, and Macau. In 1620, all the internal organs and intestines were removed and distributed to various worthy locations throughout the world, including Japan. According to I.P. Newman Fernandes in his booklet *St. Francis Xavier and Old Goa*, the corpse was examined by physicians in 1859. The report noted that:

> *Both ears are there; the right arm is missing; the left*
> *hand fingers have nails; the abdominal walls are des-*
> *iccated and a bit dark; there are no intestines. The*
> *feet are desiccated; the 5th and 4th toe of the right*
> *foot are missing. . . . [T]he body seemed to be short as*
> *compared to a normal man but this was due to some*
> *disarticulations and desiccation. The head appeared*
> *to be separated from the trunk but after verification it*
> *was found that there was no real separation.*

Xavier's body must rank as the most kissed corpse in history. It is estimated that, in one thirty-six-day period in 1922, 500,000 people kissed his remains.

The crabby arch-conservative Catholic Evelyn Waugh also got in on the act. He timed a visit to Goa in 1952 to coincide with one of the expositions of the corpse. Waugh had only praise for Xavier and paternalistic approval for the Goans:

> *From before dawn until late evening, patient queues*
> *formed and moved slowly forward to the side-door of*
> *the Cathedral. . . . Three-quarters of a million Indians*
> *were coming to thank a Spaniard, who had died far*
> *away, just 400 years ago, for their gift of Faith. . . . His*
> *beloved Goans stand guard over him and he over*
> *them. He is their single renowned passion.*

If Camoens saw Xavier's body, he made no mention of it. All

Village in South India (Kerala)

I saw was a silver casket with smudged windows. There was also a painting in which Xavier holds up a cross, gazing into it as if it were a mirror, like an effete priest guilty of the sin of vanity.

Sir Richard Francis Burton, of course, was unimpressed. Although he made no mention of visiting Xavier's tomb himself, he gleefully quotes a certain Captain Hamilton, "a sturdy old merchant militant, who infested the Eastern seas about the beginning of the eighteenth century." After visiting numerous churches in Old Goa, Hamilton "then falls foul of the *speciosa miracula* of St. Francis de Xavier. He compares the holy corpse to that of a 'new scalded pig,' [and] opines that it is a 'pretty piece of wax-work that serves to gull the people.'"

Like most of Old Goa's buildings, the Basilica of Bom Jesus was built of laterite, a porous reddish-brown stone that required regular whitewashings by a mixture of crushed clamshells to keep from crumbling due to the monsoon rains. The basilica's floor had settled, creating an undulating effect, like a chequered cloth floating on water. Everything in the basilica was out of square. It reminded me of Hagia Sophia, in Istanbul, which would already have been converted to a mosque by the time Bom Jesus was built. The basilica's *reredos* — the backdrop of the altar — was covered in gold leaf. The sunlight slanting in from the side gilded the carved cherubs, adding to the illusion of divine presence. Walking about the basilica, I noticed that the Goans had all left their footwear at the door, while the Westerners clomped about in their shoes. There is little to suggest that Camoens was particularly religious, but the cool interior would no doubt have drawn him in, as it did me, to escape the heat.

I crossed the road to Se Cathedral, where a sign warned that "Chemical Conservation Is in Progress." Se Cathedral was even larger than the Basilica of Bom Jesus, and the floor was made up entirely of gravestones. Interring corpses in the floors and walls of churches was common practice until banned due to concerns over public health. An elderly priest approached and asked me to make a donation on behalf of flood victims. He pointed out a teak donation box.

"Not for the church," he insisted. "The church has enough. I came to this conclusion in Pakistan."

"Are there a lot of Catholics in Pakistan?"

"No."

"But you were there."

"Karachi. There are Goans in Karachi. You are coming from?"

"Canada."

"Ah. I have a niece in Toronto." Again he pointed to the donation box. "A little something. For the children." The priest smiled, consulted his Rolex, and, hands folded before him, strolled silently off along one of the dim corridors.

I couldn't visit Old Goa and pass up the Convent of Saint Monica, where, in 1636, a statue of Christ on the cross is said to have opened its eyes and mouth and bled from the wounds made by the crown of thorns. I sat for half an hour in the small chapel that housed the miraculous statue. It wasn't a big statue, only half a metre tall. Since I was the only one there, I stepped up onto the altar and studied the face, expecting, well, I don't know what. I tried to imagine this 360-year-old carving coming to life, tried to imagine the people who witnessed — or thought they witnessed — the miracle. Maybe if I'd been scourging myself to the point of delirium the statue might have opened its eyes for me, or maybe if I'd eaten a ball of opium something might have happened. Straight and faithless, however, I saw only an old carving.

As with Se Cathedral, there was restoration under way at the Convent of Saint Monica. The not unpleasant smell of cement dust hung in the air, while the soothing sounds of frogs and birds filled the background, providing a chorus to the voices of the nuns echoing softly about the courtyard. My guidebook noted that "A queer nomenclature was used in this Convent: the prioress was known as *pavao* (peacock); the novice mistress as *pintasilgo* (goldfinch); the confession mistress as *pardal* (sparrow); the sacristan as *rouxinal* (nightingale); the doorkeeper as *galo* (cock), etc."

There was a story concerning Dirty Dick Burton and this convent. Some sources claimed that Burton (infamous for his erotic adventures), feeling lusty one night, broke in and kidnapped one of the nuns. Yet when he got a good look at her, he found he'd nabbed an old hag, so he shoved her in the river. In Burton's book *Goa, and the Blue Mountains,* his Goan servant Soares narrates a suspiciously similar incident about a different, unnamed, Englishman, whom he accompanied to Goa on a separate occasion. In this version, the Englishman visited the convent under the ruse of seeking a school for his sister and met a tantalizingly attractive Latin professor. With the aid of the trusty Soares, the Englishman procured a duplicate key, drugged the guards, and broke in. Unfortunately, he got lost in the convent's corridors and snatched the wrong woman. Most of Burton's biographers take this story as a veiled account of his own misadventure, one he was too fond of to edit out.

One of Dirty Dick's motives for visiting Goa was to see the *nautch* girls of Seroda. The *nautch* was an erotic Indian dance performed by girls trained from childhood. Burton mentioned that he'd been

> *reading and digesting a rich account of Seroda,*
> *which had just appeared in one of the English peri-*
> *odicals. We remembered glowing descriptions of a*
> *village, inhabited by beautiful Bayaderes [dancing*
> *girls], governed by a lady of the same class —*
> *Eastern Amazons who permitted none of the*
> *rougher sex to dwell beneath the shadow of their*
> *roof-trees. . . . We unanimously resolved to visit,*
> *without loss of time, a spot so deservedly renowned.*

Yet Burton found Seroda "dirty in the extreme" and was disappointed with the ladies: "The features were seldom agreeable. . . . They performed in sets for about four hours, concluding with the pugree, or turban dance, a peculiar performance, in which one lady takes the part of a man."

❋

As I waited for the bus back to Panjim from Old Goa, a taxi driver pulled up and leaned out the window.

"Taxi?"

"No."

"Just one hundred rupees."

"It only cost eighty to get out here."

"In rickshaw. This real car."

"I'll wait for the bus."

"Bus not coming."

"Why?"

"Bus finish."

It was about five in the afternoon. "You're lying."

"Okay, okay. Seventy."

"Nope."

"Car is good."

"Bus is better."

"Sixty."

I shook my head. It was a pleasant afternoon, the sun was easing off, I had plenty of time, and all buses led to Panjim. For once the tables were turned. The driver was stuck out here with no fare back into town. I thought of all the times in all the places, from Morocco to Turkey to India, that I'd bargained hopelessly with some indomitable driver who wouldn't give an inch. I was positively chipper.

"Fifty-five."

"No thanks."

"Fifty."

I smiled and admired the landscape.

"Forty-five."

I smiled and admired the sky.

When he dropped his price to thirty-five rupees, I was tempted, but at that point the bus arrived. I hopped aboard and paid the rupee-and-a-half fare. I'd just saved a whole dollar and even got myself a seat. As the bus rattled along the riverside road, I recalled another exchange with a driver, one from which I emerged less smug. And the issue had not been thirty rupees but one, yes, one lousy rupee. It was in Rishikesh, in northern India, the town situated where the Ganges reaches the plain. Rishikesh has two sides, one for ashrams and the other for business. I was returning from the yoga class I'd been taking each evening. Along with five Indians, I got into one of the motor rickshaws. The cost was one rupee. I knew the cost was one rupee because I'd been taking the rickshaw at least twice a day for two weeks. One rupee. I was feeling good. The weather was lovely — not cool, not hot — and, while the rickshaw was cramped, I was relaxed, and the others were amiable. We headed off down the road along the holy river, past people and cows and trucks that rushed up into our single headlight then dove by into darkness. Eventually, I rapped the ceiling to signal my stop. The driver pulled off, and I gave him a two-rupee note. He poked it into his shirt pocket and was about to drive off when I asked for my change.

"No change."

"It's one rupee."

He shook his head.

I frowned. "I took this same route two hours ago. It's one rupee."

Again he shook his head.

"It's always one rupee."

He was adamant. "Two rupee."

I tried to stay calm, but I was pissed off. This thief was ruin-

ing my yoga high. He was ripping me off for five cents. I
insisted on my rupee. He refused to hand it over. I continued
to threaten and he continued to shrug. I took down the identity
number on the front of his rickshaw — which he announced for
my benefit because it was too dark to read. None of this
worked, so I grabbed the rickshaw and rocked it like a baby
buggy, shaking it and shouting until the passengers jumped out
and the driver clung to his seat. When I finished my performance, everyone hopped back in, and they sped off with my
rupee. I hiked the hill to the guesthouse, cursing, repeating the
serial number, determined to get the bastard, to go in person
and complain, to get him chucked in jail.

If one goes to India to find oneself, what I found that night
I'd rather lose.

❅

Returning to Benaulim from Old Goa, I went down to the
beach and ate supper in a restaurant overlooking the sea. As
the sun set, everyone's attention was drawn to the horizon by
the appearance of a waterspout. It reached from the sea to the
clouds in a long wavering trumpet. Even the most jaded Goan
hands hauled out their cameras.

Benaulim had changed since 1990. There were new hotels
and an immense condo project nearing completion. This
meant a change in foreigners. Along with the old hippies, neo-
hippies, and wanna-be hippies, the backpackers, drifters, and
vagabonds, there were now elderly couples from Munich and
London and Paris. A few tables over, some middle-aged
Cockneys were loudly denouncing the local beer, Kingfisher.

Fifteenth-century public baths (Kathmandu)

One spat a mouthful into the sand, while another barked "Oi! Mustapha. Got any fish 'n' chips?" When it turned out there were no fish and chips to be had, the entire group walked out, their lobster-red legs glowing in the setting sun, and their loafers filling with sand.

When they were gone, a woman of about thirty sat down at the table. The waiter came over. In a French accent, she asked, "You have sweet lime so-dah?"

"Yes."

"I will 'ave one sweet lime so-dah."

The waiter left, and the woman lit a Gitane. She had her black hair shaved close to her skull, a braided rat tail dangling down her neck, and the lean, hard look of someone who knows things.

The waterspout had weakened but was still clearly visible. In a clever conversational opening, I pointed and said "Waterspout."

She raised sceptical eyebrows. "Comment?"

I indicated the horizon. "Waterspout."

She followed my finger. "Ah. Bon." She touched her Gitane to her lips and puffed as delicately as an angelfish kissing the glass of an aquarium.

"Been in India long?"

"Comment?"

"Been here long?"

She gazed at me and then shrugged. "Je ne comprends pas."

The waiter arrived with her sweet lime soda. "Ah," said the woman. "How much is it?"

"Ten rupees."

She gave him a ten and a two. "There is your *baksheesh.*"

"Thank you."

"You're welcome."

When the waiter was gone, the woman and I stared out at the horizon.

I now felt involved in a sociology experiment. I said to the lady with the Gitane, "Do you like Goa?"

"Excusez moi?"

"Goa. You like it?"

"Je ne parle pas Anglais."

"Ah." And with that I gave up. We both turned away to watch the waterspout wilt and the evening darken.

Next to the Israelis, the French were, in my experience, the crabbiest people on the planet. My theory is that they are forever put out by the fact that English is the lingua franca of the world. Embittered, they seem to wonder how a people like the English — who couldn't paint, cook, make wine, or make love — could have dominated the world. There were many French people in Goa. From what I could see, French men came in two types: junkie and porker. And I suppose it was a part of the mystery that is the French themselves that motivated fat middle-aged Frenchmen to stroll about in bikini briefs and carry purses. As for the French junkies, they lurked in chai shops — gaunt and ghoulish — supplementing their diet of smack with *bidis* and Coca Cola while watching for tourists to rob. As with all truths, however, I admit there are a few exceptions. One of the finest Frenchmen I ever met was a heroin addict. I got to know him in Calcutta in 1979, at the Astoria

Hotel. I'd been there a week, hogging a double room all to myself, when one afternoon the manager asked me if I'd like to share it.

"With who?"

"With him."

On the bench in reception sat a hunched Frenchman who looked more in need of a blood transfusion than a room. My enthusiasm for such a roommate was not intense. Yet my incurable cheapness got the better of me. I agreed, swayed by the thought of saving two dollars a night.

Pascal dragged his pack up to the room, crawled groaning onto the other bed, curled up in the foetal position, and hugged his stomach as if it was a wet paper bag about to split apart. I sat on my bed and watched.

It turned out that Pascal had just spent three days and three nights in the Dacca airport waiting for his Bangladesh Biman flight to Paris. He didn't step from the airport once during those seventy-two hours. Yet the plane never arrived. The Bangladeshi officials simply smiled and shrugged. Sorry, no plane. No refund, either. So Pascal spent another day and night crossing the swamps and streams of the Ganges delta to Calcutta. He'd mailed all his heroin home to his mother, in Bordeaux, sifted into postcards that he'd peeled apart and then reglued. He planned to sell the smack in France, fly to Colombia and buy cocaine, mail it home, sell it, then return to Asia. Now, his stash of smack en route to France, he was trying to kick his habit via opium. But his body wanted the hard stuff, so he spent the next week groaning on his bed.

When Pascal was feeling better, he showed me his leather

satchel specially fitted with a false bottom. He was particularly proud of it.

"I will line with 'ashish," he said, making a paving motion with his palm.

Pascal was feeling better because the elderly bellhop, Prakash, had brought him some heroin. Prakash had placed it in Pascal's palm like a fond uncle bestowing a gift of candy. Pascal was looking better too, in clean white drawstring pants, a white cotton shirt, plus a short haircut. He winked, "I throw zem off guard."

Although he moved with a slow narcotic precision, he was as lean and sharp as a syringe. The heroin he had was a variety called Malaysian rocks, and it resembled chunks of brown sugar. Pascal's dark eyes met mine. Was I interested?

Well, yes, as a matter of fact I was. And while I hadn't come to Asia with the intention of doing drugs, I did believe in Voltaire's opinion that "trying everything once is philosophy." Especially when it's free. So I snorted up. It grated like gravel up my nostrils, and I just had time to step into the bathroom and watch my vomit pour in a neat stream into the antique toilet bowl. Then I sank to the bed as if pinned to the bottom of the ocean with a thousand metres of water on my chest. I tried sitting up, but my strength was gone, and very soon so was any and all desire. Meanwhile, the veteran Pascal played solitaire with the deliberation of a tarot reader. The full context of Voltaire's dictum is worth noting. Voltaire had just spent a night indulging with the Marquis de Sade and his retinue. Voltaire had impressed them all with his enthusiasm. Yet when the marquis invited him back, Voltaire declined, saying, "trying everything once is philosophy, but twice is perversion."

I became a pervert. The tidal pull of "the urge" soon had me, and I learned how satisfying it was to give in.

"So, Grant, I think you like zee powder."

I couldn't argue. After my initiation, we became closer. There was a bond.

Pascal was a bit of a heroin philosopher, and that's one reason I liked him. "You know why I like zee powder? Because for me it feel like I am back inside my mother. I am at one."

Pascal spent day and night inside his mother. Yet, like the few really skilled alcoholics I'd known, he paced his intake so that he could function. He'd found what Malcolm Lowry called "the fine line between the shakes of too little and the abyss of too much."

I didn't do heroin out of a desire to return to the womb, nor did I do it out of despair; I did it out of curiosity. That was why I was in India. I wanted to try everything, to do everything.

Prakash got us some *ganja*, which Pascal rolled up with the heroin. I preferred this. The pot provided a glimmer that balanced the solemnity of the smack. Almost chipper, I'd descend the grotto-like stairs to Sudder Street, nod to Prakash, wave to the rickshaw wallahs, then travel on down the sidewalk past the bookseller whose row of English novels was arranged by size from large to small, beginning with three identical editions of Joyce's *Ulysses*. I'd return to the room with breakfast — two bottles of Thums Up Cola.

Pascal had studied civil engineering. He liked math. "Zee numbers feel good in my mind."

He was obsessively neat. When he finished preparing a

heroin reefer, he slotted everything away into a small teak box. Everything had to be in order, in balance, like an equation. One afternoon I returned with the Colas, and he'd counted all the tiles in the floor — but he'd forgotten the number. He was reading *Virgin Soil* by the Russian novelist Turgenev. "Listen," he said, "this is zee suicide note of T: 'I could not simplify myself.'"

Simplicity was Pascal's mantra. Heroin certainly simplified. It unplugged the frontal lobe and opened a back door to Buddhistic calm. It dumbed down the inner voice so that you sat like a stone in the sea watching the coloured fish. I liked heroin.

Pascal also had a copy of Herodotus. One afternoon he read out what the Father of Lies had to say about India, 2,500 years ago.

> *All the Indian tribes I have mentioned copulate in the open like cattle; their skins are of the same colour, much like the Ethiopians'. Their semen is not white like other people's, but black like their own skins.*

"Was Herodotus ever in India?" I asked.

"No."

"Why do you read him?"

"Because I like the fantastic."

Eventually, Pascal went to the foreigner's booking office and bought a train ticket to Delhi. From Delhi he'd fly to Paris. Back in the room, he rolled a reefer sprinkled with powder. "So, Grant. We smoke zee last one."

I was moved by his solemn sense of occasion. We were going our separate ways, and this called for a gesture, a toast. Pernod was not available, so we did the best we could.

"Your mother will be happy to see you."

Pascal considered this in his sombre way. "Yes. The house is very old, and she is alone. I must look after her. It is a son's duty." He showed me the set of opium weights he'd bought her as a present, a series of lead elephants of increasing size.

"She'll like them."

"I hope so. She always wish to visit zee East, to see zee Taj, but she is too old now. So she will see through my eyes."

I frowned. "But you didn't see the Taj."

He smiled. "I will make zee white lie. I talked to many people who have seen. It is enough. And of course I have sent her zee postcard."

I was touched by Pascal's white lie.

Then he grew solemn. "Travel is a sad joy. And now it is over."

I knew what he meant. "But you'll go to South America," I reminded him.

"Yes."

"Be careful there."

He nodded. "To buy coke is a great risk. I must trust no one."

We sat a long time listening to the street: the clink of a rickshaw wallah's handbell, the high whine of Hindi singing, horns, traffic. I walked out to the street with him. We shook hands. I hoped his mother would like the opium weights. After meeting Pascal, I looked more kindly upon junkies.

❋

The Portuguese involvement in opium was minimal compared to that of the British, at least at the production end. Until the British got hold of Hong Kong, opium entered China via the Portuguese colony of Macao.

Opium was vital to the British economy. Britain purchased vast amounts of tea from China, yet had few goods that attracted the Chinese. This meant a serious drain on Britain's silver supply. The British needed to find a commodity to trade for tea. The answer was opium, for which there was already a demand. The British can't be blamed for getting the Chinese addicted, but through organizing the growth, refinement, and sale of the drug in India they certainly worsened China's already existing problem. One study notes that "Opium thus became the chief India product upon which the [British East India] Company relied for its tea investment." Opium production in India fluctuated, but as recently as 1918 it was approximately 21,000 chests or some 1.3 million kilograms per year. Two-thirds was exported to China. The British got Hong Kong as one of the concessions following the Second Opium War of 1858, in which Britain and France forced the legalization of opium. Any moral concerns regarding the opium trade were easily outbalanced by economic ones. And in this, corrupt Chinese middlemen were as guilty as the various foreign devils.

The era of the opium clippers coincided with that of the celebrated tea clippers. One author waxed ecstatic over the glory years of the trade:

*What more thrilling task for a shipmaster than that
of outwitting wily mandarins, out-manoeuvring
Imperial war junks and out-sailing every merchant-
man, aye, and man-of-war that he encountered in
his racing passages between India and the Canton
river! Who would exchange such a life – a man's life
– for the slavery of the modern machine? Who would
not jump out of his soft bed and sling his hammock
aboard an opium clipper, could we but put the clock
back? And who of us would not prefer the hardships
and hard knocks of that forbidden trade to the soul-
destroying emptiness of our present day conditions?*

❀

A few days after visiting Old Goa, I went to Braganza House. It
was four hundred years old and in places looked it. It was
located in the village of Chandor, about twenty kilometres
inland from Benaulim. The house had been built by two brothers and was now two houses, about fifty metres long, in one.
Mr. Pereira-Braganza, the old man who showed me around his
side of the house, looked as dilapidated as his home. He was
about seventy and frail, his pants drooped, his teeth were blue
cheese, and his breath was vile. He showed me the mirrored
ballroom with its floor of Italian marble that was now as con-
cave as a soup bowl. I asked him about his ancestors and why
they'd come out from Portugal. He raised his forefinger and,
cautioning me, tipped it side to side like a metronome.

"We are Goan. We have no Portuguese blood."

"Yet your name is Portuguese."

He shrugged.

"Have you ever been to Portugal?"

Again he shook his head.

"Is life better now that the Portuguese are gone?"

He laughed bitterly. "Worse."

"How?"

"We lost all our land."

When I asked why, all he'd say, as he wandered the remnants of his family's grand past, was, "The Indian government."

I found this ironic given that his forebear, the journalist Luiz de Menezes Braganza, was a crusader for Goan independence.

He led me past lion-footed furniture of Goan teak, a crocodile skin, photos of Carmen Miranda and Elizabeth Taylor, sedan chairs, and a private chapel with silver candlesticks and a carved wooden angel bearing aloft the limp body of Christ. He also acknowledged that he had one of Saint Francis Xavier's fingernails, encrusted in diamonds, though was unable to show it to me because it was in a safety deposit box. As he led me around, we passed workmen employed in the long-overdue project of restoration. I donated one hundred rupees to the cause, and he, sleepy, returned to his beloved dust.

Mrs. Aida Menezes Braganza occupied the other side of the house. She was the granddaughter of Luiz de Menezes Braganza. Like her side of the mansion, she was in much better shape than her relative next door. In her seventies, she was bright and neat and gracious, her teeth were clean, and her English was good. She had been to Portugal many times, she said as she led me around the house. Her grandfather's library was intact and included two editions of the *Encyclopaedia Britannica*, the thirteenth and fourteenth, the latter, for some reason, shelved upside down. As we walked, Mrs. Braganza pointed to lamps, tables, and floors and gave their age and history.

"These two vases are from China. That inlaid bureau is from Japan. Those lamps are from Macao. The floor here is only three hundred years old. The tiles are from Venice. This bed is four hundred years old, made here in Goa. The spread is from China, yes, and this spread over here I made myself." She touched a crocheted white bed cover of impressive detail. "I finished it just eight days ago. Two months it took me. Now," she continued, leading me across the room, "this brass bed was made in Bristol, England. It is just one hundred and fifty years old."

Eventually, we stood before a painting of one of her great-grandfathers, that would have fitted seamlessly into any Portuguese family archive, right down to the Napoleonic haircut, the high-collared coat, and the fair complexion. Wondering if her relative next door got it wrong, I repeated the question about why her family had left Portugal.

"We are not from Portugal. We are from right here." She stated this with defiance and pride.

As we stood before the portrait, a tall man in his forties passed along the corridor, barefoot, wearing gold basketball shorts and a T-shirt. He nodded. This was her son, home for a visit from Sao Paulo, Brazil, where he worked. Before I could talk to him, he disappeared through a door and was gone.

"What does your son do?"

"He is in business."

"What sort of business?"

But she directed my attention to a Scottish cookie tin with a painted scene of a girl reclining beneath a tree with a lamb. "A friend sent this from Edinburgh last year."

When I left I felt like I'd stepped directly from Portugal to India in one stride. From the road, Braganza House looked like it was being swallowed by vegetation. Still, it was in far finer shape today than when John (no relation to Jan) Morris visited it in the mid-1960s. At that time the house had only been reoccupied for a few years, after having been shut up for thirteen. According to Morris, a former officer in the Indian army,

> *Cobwebs were everywhere, and as we started to ascend the once grand staircase, now stripped of its finery, I felt as though I was entering a house of the dead. . . . I became more and more depressed as we wandered from room to room, all dust-covered and smelling of decay. There was a great deal of very beautiful convoluted carved furniture, made in Goa from Portuguese designs, many occasional tables of like design, and dozens of chairs in the style of Hepplewhite. A narrow salon, like the long gallery in an English noble house, ran the entire length of the building. . . . Beyond the salon was a dining room, with a table and chairs to seat one hundred people, but the roof had leaked and rain had discoloured the walls. The house had neither electricity nor running water.*

The other side of the house was, at the time, in a similar state. "The corridor gave on to a large room containing a huge four-poster bed with very dirty sheets and a disordered newspaper. Our guide apologized for the state of the room. He had, he said, only just risen, although it was now late afternoon."

＊

I couldn't leave Goa without visiting the Rodrigueses again. It was noon when I arrived, the same crowd of Goan men sat playing cards and drinking, and Ezelita sat as still as a shrub.

"I'm going to Cochin."

Her expression didn't change. "Cochin."

"Yes. Have you been?"

"No."

"No?"

"Cochin is in India?"

"Yes."

She nodded, as if it was good that Cochin was in India.

I asked her what I'd been asking everyone else. "Has Goa changed?"

"Change?"

"Is it better now that the Portuguese are gone?"

"Better? No better. Worse."

"But there's been development."

Now she seemed to wake up. "Development? Look at these boy." She pointed to the men playing cards. "What good is dewelopment if there are no job? Only Hindu get job."

"Will your son go back to the Gulf?"

She turned and considered him. He was drunk, his singlet

stained and sweaty, his hand full of cards as limp and grubby as two-rupee notes. "I don't know. They are asking."

"For him?"

"Yes."

"For him to come back?"

"Yes."

"That's good."

"But he is drinking too much."

We contemplated this in silence. Outside a faint breeze moved the trees, but it offered no relief from the heat.

"How is Monica?"

"Monica?" Ezelita spoke as if the name was foreign to her.

"Is she here?"

"Not here. Out."

"She goes out a lot?"

"Not so much."

"Oh."

Ezelita did not offer to expand on the subject. There was another silence. Silence didn't seem to bother her; she seemed completely comfortable with it. I wasn't, so I found myself trying to come up with more questions. Surely this couldn't be it? I wanted to remind Ezelita of the job application I'd once written for Monica. I wanted to remind her of going to church with her and her family, of Carnival, of Valentine's Day. A few years earlier I'd even written them a letter. It was no use asking whether they'd ever received it. I tried thinking of something else to say. I knew that once I was gone I'd come up with all kinds of questions and comments, but at that moment I couldn't think of anything. So Ezelita and I just sat there in the stupefying heat, the afternoon as silent as a stagnant pool.

Walking back along the road, not far from the Rodrigues's, I saw a woman coming toward me. She was carrying a chicken by its legs, swinging it idly, as if she had nowhere to go. She looked thirtyish, pretty, plump, and she wore a frock, meaning she was most likely Catholic. As we got nearer, she looked up from her feet, and our eyes met. We watched each other. We slowed down as if to speak. Then we continued on by.

※

When I got back to the hotel in Benaulim, I discovered that the room next to mine was now occupied. Chantal was from Avignon, and Paulo was from Rome. Chantal was reading Kundera's *The Unbearable Lightness of Being*, while Paulo fried garlic and onions over a Coleman stove set up on the concrete porch we shared. They invited me to supper. Chantal and Paulo were in their forties, both were deeply tanned and weathered, and they wore a lot of Indian jewelry. They said they came to Goa every year. As we talked, we watched Paulo add noodles to boiling water, then roll a small wheel of Parmesan from his pack, cut a wedge, and begin grating it.

Chantal smiled. "Wherever he go he must have Italian cheese, herbs, and espresso."

Paulo laid out four plates just as a woman came up the steps and joined us. This was Marika. She was Austrian, looked about thirty-five, wore a dress that looked like it came from a Salvation Army sale and old pumps cracked at the toes, and had her dirty blonde hair in tight braids. She was conspicuously free of jewelry and tattoos. For some reason I thought of Lama Yeshe. Like him, Marika was impressive more by what she didn't have than by what she had.

Paulo served up the spaghetti. We added Parmesan and pepper, and, as the dusk purpled the sky, we ate in silence, listening to the rising rhythm of the cicadas. Later Paulo made coffee, and we began to share stories of our travels in India. It turned out that Marika had been in India for six straight years.

"I go a triangle," she said. "Goa, Varanasi, Dharamsala. In Goa I make sandals. In Varanasi I make bags and belts. In Dharamsala I make cheese."

She said she'd married a sadhu three years previously and walked with him from Lucknow to Puri, about one thousand kilometres. "Then, I don't know, he goes crazy. He beat me. I leave." She sounded more perplexed than depressed.

"You didn't go home then?" I asked.

She looked shocked. She insisted she'd never return to Austria. "The people are like motors."

"What do you mean?"

"They are made of metal. They are machine."

She'd recently spent six months on her own in Pakistan. By wearing a burka, a traditional garment that turned women into tents, she hadn't had any problems. She shrugged. "The people are good. It was the fruit season. The mountain they smelled of apricot."

❋

I decided to go south, to Cochin, where the Portuguese had
established themselves before taking Goa. Despite the fact that
Indian Airlines once enjoyed the honour of having the second
worst safety record in the world, I bought a ticket and a few
days later boarded a 707. The state of the plane didn't inspire
confidence. Everything was grubby and torn. The carpets were
peeling up, the seats were ripped, the plastic window shades
were blackened with grime, the lavatory was filthy, and, to top
it off, the elderly man next to me occupied himself the entire
flight by swallowing air and burping it back up. I don't know,
maybe this was some kind of ayurvedic exercise, but it bugged
me, so, since the plane was only half full, I moved to another
seat. The stewardesses, meanwhile, glided regally up and
down the aisles passing out stale candies.

It was the first domestic flight I'd ever taken in India, so I'd
got to the airport early. In the departure lounge, I'd watched an
elderly Indian reach into his shirt pocket, take out money,
count it, fold it, and return it to the pocket. He then stretched
out his right leg so that he could reach into his right front
pocket, took out more money, counted it, folded it, and
returned it to the pocket. Next he stretched out his left leg and
reached into his front left pocket, took out a wad of bills,
counted it, folded it, and returned it to the pocket. He repeated
this exercise with both his back pockets. Finally, he reached
down and tugged up his trouser leg, pulled a flap of notes from
his sock, counted it, folded it, and returned it to his sock. After
that, apparently satisfied, he opened a newspaper and read.

Waiting there to board the flight, I found myself studying
the body language of the people around me. Two German

women entered looking harried, their shoulders bare, their armpits bushy, their shins unshaven. They moved like oxen, utterly without composure, utterly lacking the deportment Indian women seem to have studied all their lives. Maybe such a studied manner was a bad thing; maybe it was a sort of psychological foot binding. It was attractive, though, especially when seen in contrast to the Westerners who trundled in gawking and gaping like cattle.

From the air, Cochin looked low and swampy. It was just one in a cluster of islands and turned out to be far more humid than Goa. In fact, Goa was almost arid in comparison. When I stepped from the plane, the damp draped itself across my face like a wet wool muffler. It was immediately obvious that Cochin was a place that rotted even as it grew, a place where it would be easy to catch some disease that would cause colourful moulds and fungi to sprout and blossom inside your nasal passages and deep in your lungs, a place where cuts would flourish and infections ripen.

While Old Goa had Saint Francis Xavier's corpse, Cochin had, or at one time had, Vasco da Gama's. Da Gama died in Cochin in 1524, during his third stay in India. He'd returned in the position of viceroy, with the mission to clean up the Portuguese colonies, because their reputation for corruption had finally reached Lisbon. The fearless da Gama was the man for the job. When his fleet was hit by a submarine earthquake just off the coast of India, his response was to gather his crew around him and announce, "Friends, rejoice and be happy, for even the sea trembles before us." Once ashore, he set about making changes. Finding men using the hospital in

Old Goa as a hotel, he drove them all out. According to the historian Henry Hart, da Gama "Forebade the hospital to receive anyone wounded in a brawl. Crews of ships were to remain aboard while in harbour and receive their rations there." Despite his reputation for cruelty, he was nonetheless welcomed back to Goa. He was now fifty-five years old, had "a florid complexion, with somewhat Israelitish features, large eyes, heavy eyebrows, hooked nose, and a beard, which in his later years was white." But, on a mission south to Cochin, the climate proved too much even for him. He died and was buried in St. Francis church, where his corpse spent fourteen years before being dug up and returned to Lisbon.

I got a room at the Grace Tourist Home for 150 rupees, a fairly pain-free five US dollars, hung my mosquito net, took off all my clothes, stretched out on the bed beneath the fan, and sweated. The fan, whirring full speed, caused the mosquito net to thrash as if in a hurricane, but still I was soaked. Lying there I realized something – I really didn't like the heat. In fact, I hated it. I felt lethargic and ill, which was the reason I never went into steam rooms or saunas. I preferred a temperate climate. And, always wanting to be somewhere else no matter where I was, I became nostalgic for a December once spent in Rome – the air cool but not cold, the sun welcome instead of oppressive, and the light coaxing the colours from the leaves and the stained glass of the cathedrals.

Cochin has been called the Venice of the East, along with Bangkok and a few similar swamps that shared a history of marshes and malaria. Spices from Indonesia and Malacca and

Chinese fishing nets (Cochin)

Ceylon were depoted in Cochin and traded onward to the markets of East Africa, Egypt, and Europe. In the Middle Ages, pepper and sandalwood from Cochin would have spent time in Venetian warehouses. When da Gama reached Cochin, it was a cosmopolitan city, with a population that included Hindus, Muslims, Christians (who traced their roots back to 52 AD and the Apostle Thomas), and Jews. Cochin had India's oldest synagogue, a street called Jew Road, and an area listed on the maps as Jew Town. Until the fifteenth century, Chinese junks sailed to Cochin. The Chinese introduced Cochin's famous Chinese fishing nets that still line the waterfront.

I went to take a look at those fishing contraptions and found I was in luck. It was high tide, and the nets were in full swing. Each consisted of a net the size of a parachute stretched on a frame of telephone-pole-sized beams, all of which was counterbalanced by a rope tied with keg-sized stones. The net was lowered into the sea for ten minutes at a time, and then four or five men raised it by hauling on the rope in the manner of sailors hoisting a sail. The ocean along here was thick with plants that looked like lilies. Enormous trees shaded the seawall, and cafés featured crates of freshly caught fish that they'd fry up right there for you. Freighters passed, and small wood-hulled ferries travelled between Vypin Island, Willingdon Island, and Ernakulum.

Cochin's architecture reflected a strong European presence. Whereas contemporary Indian architecture fell into two categories, the hut and the block house, many buildings in Cochin were European-looking, with inclined roofs and ornamental woodworking. The Portuguese arrived in 1498, the

Dutch took it away from them in 1663, the British took it from the Dutch in 1795, and all left their mark on the architecture.

※

I went to bed early my first night in Cochin, wearing earplugs to mute the roar of the fan, but the plugs were no match for the music that began to blare from a nearby Hindu temple at four-thirty in the morning. It lasted half an hour, at which point a muezzin from a nearby mosque took over, calling the Muslims to prayer. I went onto the porch and sat in the predawn light. A couple of joggers trotted past. It was almost cool at this time of day. Almost. I turned off the fan and listened to the muezzin's voice. In that delicious lull before the day erupted full and hot and frantic, I thought how much more impressive the muezzin would be if it wasn't a recording, and a bad recording at that.

I spent the day wandering the area listed on my map as Jew Town. It was populated by spice merchants. At times, my eyes stung from the dust of pepper and cardamom. A flatbed truck blocked the narrow street. I watched men loading it with forty-kilo rice sacks. They gripped the sacks by the corners and heaved them up. I knew this kind of heavy work from my years at a mass-production bakery in Vancouver, except instead of sacks of rice it was sacks of flour that we unloaded from boxcars.

After looking at the synagogue and the Dutch palace, I met a Spanish woman named Magdalena, from Granada. This intrigued me, for over the years, I'd seriously considered giving Granada a try as a place to live, because it was beautiful, there was work, and it had history. Magdalena announced that there was a conspiracy among the Arabs to retake the old part of Granada.

"Is true. They find drunks and make them a deal. If they convert to Islam, they set them up in business."

Magdalena was about thirty, had her black hair piled in a bun on top of her head, and chain-smoked Marlboros.

"You've seen this?"

"I live in Granada! Men who last year they are begging for drinks, now the bastards they own shops. Five times a day they are praying to Allah. It is a cabal."

"They built the Alhambra."

"So the British can come back and claim India because they built VT station? Or the Portuguese can say Goa belongs to them?"

"Not exactly."

She moved on to a more pressing subject. "Do you have any hash?"

"Hash? No."

"I need some hash." She looked around as if she might find some on the ground. "Is too fucking humid here. Granada is too fucking cold, and this place is too fucking humid. I'm sweating. I hate sweating. I'm getting dehydrated. Is danger-ous. I could get heat stroke. But you can't drink the water."

"Bottled water is cheap."

"But I've heard they put tap water in the bottles and reseal them. So I'm living on Coca Cola. I hate Coca Cola."

"What do you think of India?"

"It's like the air. The air is polluted, but I need to breathe."

"And Cochin?"

"Cochin!" She shut her eyes as if now I'd really gone and asked a dumb question. "I'm worried. The monkeys ate my malaria pills."

"Monkeys?"

"Last week. In Mahabaleshwar. They climb into my room. All my malaria pills. Gone. Like candy. And then they — " she made a gouging motion with her hands. "They tear the mattress all up. The hotel man make me buy a new one." And with that she stalked off.

❁

That evening I contemplated the fact that my trip was nearly over, a source of relief, but also one of doubt. What next? Or more to the point, where next? Latin America? Africa? Maybe it didn't matter. As the Spanish proverb says, "He who would bring home the wealth of the Indies, must carry the wealth of the Indies with him." Camoens had certainly done that. I went to a small restaurant surrounded by a hedge of flowers and infested with mosquitoes. While trying to eat and slap at the same time, I met a German named Willy. If Marika the Austrian held the record for consecutive years spent in India, Willy the German held the record for having been more places than anyone I'd ever met. He'd spent two years in Australia and three cycling throughout South America. He'd cycled across Canada and the United States. He'd biked from Tijuana to Panama, spent three years in Africa, been to Mauritius and the Seychelles, spent six months in China, cycled Indonesia, and was now on his second trip through India. He was only thirty-seven, but the kilometres were there on his pitted face despite his lean, athletic build. He wore a perpetual frown and needed a shave; even when he laughed he frowned. We traded stories, and eventually he told me about a train journey in Zimbabwe.

The night before departure, the stationmaster told Willy the train was scheduled to leave at eight the next morning. An old Africa hand, Willy slept long and well and reached the station at 10 a.m. As he'd expected, the train hadn't even arrived. He returned at noon. No train. He went for lunch and came back. No train. He sat down to wait, and at five a train chugged in. But it was the wrong one. At eight in the evening, he paid a small boy to come and tell him if the train arrived, and he went off to have a supper of guinea pig and beer. He returned. Still no train. Finally, at midnight, the train bored its way out of the darkness behind its headlight and stood hissing and sighing in the station. Willy fought his way on and, to his amazement, got a bunk. He took a Valium and slept until six in the morning. When he woke he looked out the window and found the train hadn't moved; they were still in the station. By nine, the compartment was packed, and the African sun had turned it into a fire box. Three hours later, twenty-eight hours late, they pulled out. An hour later they broke down. They sat for yet another hour. He put his head out the window, looked up and down the track, and saw people sitting in the scrub cooking lunch. He climbed down and walked to the front of the train. The engineer and some others had their heads on the tracks, dozing.

"What's going on?"

"We waiting for help."

Willy returned to his compartment. At five, an engine arrived and hauled them on to the next town, two hours away. There he was informed that there were no more trains, that in fact the tracks ended. Determined to continue, he set out walking the same night. He walked ten days, from village to village.

"How was it?" I asked.

"The best experience of my life."

"But no more trains. Now you're on a bicycle."

"Yes."

"The hills must be hard."

"No. It's not the hills. It's the wind." He frowned, beaten. "I hate wind. But I must go on." He set his elbows hard on his knees and stared past me, like a man dwelling sorrowfully on his fate.

"Will you keep on travelling?"

He turned his hands palms upward and shrugged. "What else can I do?"

"I don't know. Get married?"

He blew air and shook his head. "Twice already I am married."

I didn't know what to say, so I told my train wreck story.

❋

Had I met Willy a few weeks later, I'd have had a cheerier train story to tell, one that to me crystallized India's eccentric allure and reflected a country simultaneously medieval and modern, European and Asian, that employed ox carts and computers and that in twenty-five years would be the most populated

country on the planet. It's the train ride I like to remember
India by, the train ride I remember more fondly than any
other, and it is the story with which I will end this book. It took
place on the Lalbagh Express, from Madras to Bangalore.

I was sitting in the second-class day coach, thinking about
my travels. After five trips in twenty years, I'd seen Goa twice,
interviewed people, seen churches and temples, ventured out
to the desert, gone up into the mountains, seen the east coast
and the west coast, and visited the south. I hadn't stayed as
long as Camoens, but I'd covered more ground. And more
than anything else, India had satisfied my deep urge to travel
as far from home as possible. Now I just had a few days before
I was scheduled to fly out, so I decided to give Bangalore and
Mysore a quick visit.

Waiting for the train to pull out of Madras, I looked around
and noticed that all the other passengers were reading. Across
the aisle a young Indian woman read a Perry Mason novel.
Next to her an elderly man read *India Today*, and virtually
everyone else read a magazine called *MOVIE*. None of that
Third World train business here, with the chickens and goats
and the beggars playing violins made from bleach bottles and
fence wire. No, it was Perry Mason and *MOVIE*, plus three guys
and a bottle of Johnnie Walker Black Label. They were well-
dressed but drunk. Not a welcome sight. The prospect of a
four-hour train trip with these booze louts made me want to
jump off. I especially worried about one of them. Drunker
than the rest, he positioned himself behind me while his two
buddies plunked themselves down on the bench facing mine.
When the drunk shouted across my shoulder, "Are those our

fucking seats?" I figured I was in for a major confrontation with three Indians who had a hate-on for Whitey.

One of his friends, however, immediately distinguished himself as a philosopher. He responded in a professorial manner. "What do you think?"

This created a moment of pause. "Well, then, what the fuck am I doing over here?" His tone implied that someone — certainly not him — had screwed up. He groped his way around and sat with his friends opposite me. He had rings on all his fingers, shoulder-length hair, a mango-coloured shirt open to the navel, and a brass medallion. His name was Kapoor; his companions called him Krap.

Krap draped his arm around Harb, a dour, paunchy pal who stared out the window. Harb shrugged Krap off. Harb had clearly had enough of Krap's antics. Krap turned his attention to Harb's ample thigh and squeezed it, gauging the flab.

"You better start doing your Jane Fonda, man."

Harb stared harder out the window, wishing the train would hurry up and pull out.

"Harb's getting homesick," said Krap to the philosopher. "Don't worry Harb. Soon you will be home in your very own fart sack."

Harb exhaled heavily and continued glaring out the window.

Now a man came down the aisle selling chai.

Krap bought a cup, ceremonially poured its contents out the window, then filled it with whiskey. "What time is it?"

The philosopher leaned to read the watch on Krap's wrist. "Four-thirty."

Krap was delighted. "Four-thirsty!" He gulped his drink.

The philosopher said, "Because you are my friend, I will give you some advice."

Krap put his hand to his heart and said, in a whiskey wheeze, "So happy to know I am loved."

"Don't drink on an empty stomach." He passed Krap a cookie.

"What the fuck is this?"

"Sugar and something brown."

Krap dropped it out the window, then discovered Harb lighting a cigarette. "Please don't smoke, sir. You are polluting my atmosphere."

Harb inhaled hard and said nothing.

"What is your fucking problem, man?" said Krap.

The philosopher sat back, crossed his legs, and smoothed his trousers over his knee. "Why don't you develop some new phrases? Fucking this, fucking that, what is your fucking problem. These are getting a bit stale."

Krap didn't hear because he was lighting a cigarette. Then he grabbed the seat, shouting in terror "Are we moving?"

The philosopher said, "Does it feel as if we are moving?"

"Yes."

"Then we are moving."

The train had not budged.

A one-armed beggar presented a framed plaque for inspection and, hopefully, some money. Krap read it with interest. Then he read it aloud, in whatever language it was they spoke here.

The philosopher nodded his approval. The phrasing was

apparently eloquent. "Upanishads."

"Up whose?" asked Krap. He returned the plaque and made a comment.

The beggar liked it. He laughed loudly, and his stump flew up as if he meant to slap his thigh in delight.

"Here's a buck." Krap gave him a rupee. Then Krap rediscovered Harb, aimed his finger like a pistol, and suggested Harb's undies were too tight.

The philosopher imitated Krap's gesture. "Do you know the logic of this?"

Krap stared big-eyed.

"A gun. You are putting a gun to our poor Harb's head. Better you should point it at yourself." And here the philosopher turned his own finger toward his own temple, then pulled the trigger.

Krap winced, then quickly poured more whiskey, at which point the train pulled out with such a lurch that it made him spill the drink. Cursing, Krap dragged his shirt up and sucked the alcohol from it while most of the people on the train, including the woman reading the Perry Mason novel, watched.

Next Krap reached over and plucked at Harb's zipper, constructing a cone over his crotch. "What are you dreaming about you bugger?"

Harb brushed his hand away.

The philosopher said, "You think filth, you talk filth, you associate filth, ergo you are filth."

Krap stared. "I need to leak."

"So leak."

"No. First I want to say something serious."

The philosopher sat back and folded his hands. "We are waiting."

"We should have got another fucking bottle." Krap held the scotch bottle up and studied the dapper little man strutting across the label.

The train was rolling swiftly now. We were leaving Madras behind. The philosopher intoned that there was but one God, and his name was Johnnie Walker.

Krap raised the bottle in salute and swirled the last half inch. "True. But there's not enough of him to go around." He guzzled the rest.

"You are a lush."

Krap didn't argue. Mouth open, he held the upended bottle high, waiting for the final drops. Then he dangled the bottle out the window and let it fall. A faint pop was immediately lost in the racketing night, and that, it seemed, was that.

We rolled on. Soon, lulled by the booze and the rhythm and the deepening darkness, Krap's eyelids sank.

Now Harb spoke for the first time. "His liver's going to explode."

"That would be a mess." The philosopher caught my eye, gauging my reaction to all this. He was smiling slightly. They hadn't said a word to me the whole time, and I'd said nothing to them. It was an agreement we'd somehow reached. They were a travelling road show, and the entire train was the audience.

Two hours later, still kilometres from Bangalore, the train slowed to a crawl, and Krap woke. For the next hour we crept along, and Krap grew anxious. He stood, he sat, he paced. He counted backward from one hundred out loud but kept losing his spot and having to start again.

The philosopher watched with professional interest. "You must calm yourself."

"Calm myself?"

"Do yoga."

Krap frowned furiously. "Yoga?"

"Touch your toes."

Krap looked down and pointed. "They're too far away."

"Then sit."

Krap sat, crossed his ankle over his knee, and gripped his sandalled foot. "Like this?"

"Excellent. You are progressing well."

Yet yoga wasn't working, and Krap continued to grow frantic at the sluggish pace. Finally, on the outskirts of Bangalore, he ran down the aisle to the door and jumped. Harb and I watched through the window as Krap rolled down the gravel slope.

The philosopher asked, "Is he gone?"

Harb sat back and lit a cigarette. "Gone." They sat in silence. The train chugged slowly on through the night. "It's peaceful," said Harb.

"It is," agreed the philosopher. "But I suppose we better go collect him."

And both made their way to the door and jumped too.

GOLDEN GOA

Camoens reached Portugal on Friday, April 7, 1570, after a seventeen-year absence. Yet the ship, the Santa Clara, *was met not with fanfare but with the news that Lisbon was besieged by plague. Everyone was to stay aboard the ship. The quarantine lasted two weeks. Then the plague abated, and the king, in celebration, ordered every citizen to place a lighted candle in their window. When Camoens finally did step ashore, it was to a Lisbon lit up like a cathedral. At the time, it was the most important city in Europe but was already teetering toward a long decline. Its imbalance was reflected in the young king, Dom Sebastian, sixteen years old, morbid, inbred, and obsessed with the dream of leading a Crusade to drive the Muslim infidel out of North Africa. Camoens knew that Sebastian's approval was needed to get* The Lusiads *the publicity imperative to achieving a wide audience. So Camoens, pragmatic, added thirteen stanzas celebrating Sebastian in the first canto. The remaining hurdle was consent from the Board of the Holy Office of the Inquisition. Camoens went before Frei Bartolameu Ferreira, the Board's chief censor, though not before adding another stanza declaring that all the gods mentioned in the work were nothing but fantasies. Frei Bartolameu went along with Sebastian and gave his approval, no doubt aware that it was risky to disagree with a mad king.* The Lusiads *made it into print in 1572.*

Its genius was recognized immediately. And though the

jealous were swift to attack it, Camoens was awarded a pension, but it was so small that he was soon reduced once again to hack work for survival. Portugal too was in a desperate financial state made worse by natural disasters. There was a massive flood in 1572, a famine in 1574, an earthquake in 1575. The mad Sebastian was not helping. He borrowed money to assemble a fleet of thirty ships to aid the king of France against the Turks, but a storm destroyed every one while still anchored in the Tagus. Then in 1578 Sebastian invaded Morocco, was trounced, and got himself as well as some eight thousand Portuguese soldiers killed. In 1580 Portugal fell under the control of Spain, and the same year the penniless Camoens died of plague. Along with other victims of the pestilence, he was laid coffinless and without ceremony in the charnel house beneath the Church of the Franciscan Sisters of Santa Ana.

Printed and bound
in Boucherville, Quebec, Canada by
MARC VEILLEUX IMPRIMEUR INC.
in March, 2000